Praise for **Change Their Mind**

'Packed with great insights, this will make you think, laugh – and produce great results. It's such a fun read that you barely notice how much you are actually learning.'

Jack Nasher, Professor of Leadership and Organisation, Munich Business School; author of *Convinced!*

'We're all so busy shouting at each other, we never listen anymore. Who knows, if we did maybe there's more to agree on than we imagine. Horton's book gives us some very clear practical steps on how to get our point across better. We'd do well if we gave it a try.'

Iain Dale, presenter of the evening show on LBC Radio; one of Britain's leading political commentators; author of *Why Can't We All Just Get Along. . .*

'*Change Their Mind* draws on the methods of hostage negotiators, political campaigners and counsellors who work successfully with the toughest of patients. It's very practical and full of stories that show exactly how these same methods work in everyday life too.'

Lord Daniel Finkelstein OBE, Associate Editor of *The Times*; author of *Everything in Moderation*

'This book is so full of wisdom on how to communicate actively for a life full of collective wellbeing – and so engaging – you won't realise you have absorbed it! Yoda had been my guide on the fact that all our problems and potentials stem from just two emotions: love and fear. Now I have proper references for this and so much else thanks to Simon's work.'

Dr Victoria Hurth, Fellow of University of Cambridge's Institute for Sustainability Leadership

'As social creatures, humans are always trying to persuade others. Simon Horton's book will give you the tools you need to influence others effectively and ethically by finding collaborative outcomes. It's a practical and enjoyable way to be a more effective human.'

Paul Zak, Professor of Neuroscience at Claremont Graduate University; Co-Founder of Immersion Neuroscience; author of *The Moral Molecule*

'This is the kind of book the world needs right now. If we all followed these very practical tips, the world would be a much better place.'

Waj Khan, Director, UK and International Dispute Avoidance and Resolution, Prime Dispute

'In my work as a negotiator, I've seen that most people practice Maslow's famous observation: "When the only tool you have is hammer, every problem looks like a nail", trying to persuade using shouting, manipulating, and even lying. Horton's new book offers a significantly richer toolbox: how to persuade through listening, collaboration, and various other techniques, in business, at home and even with your annoying friend who supports the other political party. A must-read book very relevant to our current global context!'

Moty Crystal, CEO of NEST Negotiation Strategies; Professor of Negotiation Dynamics, Moscow School of Management SKOLKOVO.

'The quality of our life and business is the quality of our communication. We communicate and "negotiate" almost all day and every day, whether it be a business deal, a pay rise or just getting your kids to tidy up their room. This book has a comprehensive range of easy-to-understand and practical examples of how everyone can improve all areas of their lives. It will benefit everyone who reads it.'

Brian Peters, Mr Universe; CEO and Founder of The Ultimate Financial Consultant and 'Get Referrals Every Time'; author of *Transforming Your Life*

Change Their Mind

At Pearson, we believe in learning – all kinds of learning for all kinds of people. Whether it's at home, in the classroom or in the workplace, learning is the key to improving our life chances.

That's why we're working with leading authors to bring you the latest thinking and best practices, so you can get better at the things that are important to you. You can learn on the page or on the move, and with content that's always crafted to help you understand quickly and apply what you've learned.

If you want to upgrade your personal skills or accelerate your career, become a more effective leader or more powerful communicator, discover new opportunities or simply find more inspiration, we can help you make progress in your work and life.

Every day our work helps learning flourish, and wherever learning flourishes, so do people.

To learn more, please visit us at **www.pearson.com/uk**

The Financial Times

With a worldwide network of highly respected journalists, *The Financial Times* provides global business news, insightful opinion and expert analysis of business, finance and politics. With over 500 journalists reporting from 50 countries worldwide, our in-depth coverage of international news is objectively reported and analysed from an independent, global perspective.

To find out more, visit **www.ft.com**

Change Their Mind

Six steps to persuade anyone, anytime

Simon Horton

Harlow, England • London • New York • Boston • San Francisco • Toronto • Sydney • Dubai • Singapore • Hong Kong
Tokyo • Seoul • Taipei • New Delhi • Cape Town • São Paulo • Mexico City • Madrid • Amsterdam • Munich • Paris • Milan

PEARSON EDUCATION LIMITED
KAO Two
KAO Park
Harlow CM17 9NA
United Kingdom
Tel: +44 (0)1279 623623
Web: www.pearson.com/uk

First edition published 2022 (print and electronic)

ISBN: 978-1-292-40679-4 (print)
978-1-292-40678-7 (PDF)
978-1-292-40677-0 (ePub)

British Library Cataloguing-in-Publication Data
A catalogue record for the print edition is available from the British Library

Library of Congress Cataloging-in-Publication Data
A catalog record for the print edition is available from the Library of Congress

10 9 8 7 6 5 4 3 2 1
26 25 24 23 22

Cover design by Two Associates
Cover image © IIIerlok_Xolms/iStock/Getty Images Plus/Getty Images
Print edition typeset in 9/13pt Melior Com by Straive
Printed by Ashford Colour Press Ltd, Gosport

NOTE THAT ANY PAGE CROSS REFERENCES REFER TO THE PRINT EDITION

Contents

About the author

Courtesy Sam Armstrong. Used with permission.

Simon is a world-leading expert in the fields of negotiation and influence. He has taught hostage negotiators, solicitors at some of the most prestigious law firms and senior executives at some of the most successful companies in the world. He is also a visiting lecturer at Imperial College.

He lives in London, enjoys scuba-diving and cycling and he still wants to be a footballer when he grows up.

Publisher's acknowledgements

7–8 Anne Nusselder: Anne Nusselder, OpfrisDame – Freshen-Up Girl! The OpfrisDamen bring improvised theatre to festivals, corporate functions and care homes for the elderly. Anne teaches (visual) storytelling and presentation at the University of Arts Utrecht; **12–13 Vitas Poshk:** Vitas Poshkus, founder of PVA Developments, a design-orientated construction company specialising in bespoke residential projects for private clients; **17–19 Igor Rybakov:** Igor Rybakov, serial entrepreneur, venture capitalist, philanthropist, on the list of the world's richest people according to Forbes. He is co-founder of the Technonikol corporation, and founder of the Rybakov Foundation and the Rybakov Prize (called by Forbes the 'Nobel Prize in Education') and the X10 Academy, a school for entrepreneurs; **24 Reed Hastings:** Quoted by Reed Hastings; **24 Geoff Mulgan:** Quoted by Geoff Mulgan; **27–29 Jenny Radcliffe:** Jenny Radcliffe, social engineer, human factor security expert, people hacker. Jenny uses her expertise in non-verbal communication, deception and persuasion techniques for ethical white hat hacking to help secure client sites and protect them from malicious attacks. She was part of the special operations unit for the successful Channel 4 series 'Hunted'; **40–41 Patrick Fagan:** Patrick Fagan, behavioural scientist, visiting lecturer at three London universities, The author of *Hooked: Why cute sells... and other marketing magic that we just can't resist* (Pearson). Previously Lead Psychologist at Cambridge Analytica, he is currently Chief Scientific Officer at behavioural science consultancy Capuchin; **44–45 Lynda Bourne:** Dr Lynda Bourne, stakeholder engagement expert, lecturer at Monash University and Director of Professional Development at Mosaic Project Services. She is a recognised international authority on stakeholder management and visualisation technologies, publishing papers in many academic and professional journals on the topic; **47–49 David Landsman:** David Landsman, former positions include British Ambassador to Greece, British Ambassador to Albania, Managing Director of Tata Ltd (Europe) and Director of UK India Business Council. An international negotiator and expert in corporate strategy and geopolitics, he is currently Chairman of Cerebra Global Strategy and Chairman of the British-Serbian Chamber of Commerce; **62–63 Nargis Begum:** Aliya is a barrister and works as an in-house legal counsel for an investment bank. Used with permission; **66–68 Sue Atkins:** Sue Atkins, The Parenting Coach. Sue is the Parenting Expert on ITV's 'This Morning' programme as well as BBC Radio, Disney Junior, Good Morning Britain and a host of other shows on television across the world. She has been a Parenting Coach for over 15 years; **73–74 Michael Reddington:** Michael Reddington, Certified Forensic Interviewer, Developer of the Disciplined Listening Method, President of InQuasive, Inc. Michael is an expert at moving people from resistance to commitment. He has spent over a decade training investigators on the successful application of non-confrontational interview and interrogation techniques; **82–83 Richard Bryant-Jefferies:** Richard Bryant-Jefferies, counsellor and author. Richard has spent many years counselling and supervising counselling in various settings, specialising in addiction counselling. He has written over 20 books on the topic and numerous chapters in other professional books; **98–100 David Owen:** Lord David Owen, Foreign Secretary 1977–1979 and MP for Plymouth for 26 years. He also held posts as Navy Minister and Health Minister and was co-founder of the Social Democratic Party and its Leader from 1983–87 and 1988–90. From 1992–95, he served as EU peace negotiator in the former Yugoslavia and co-authored the Vance-Owen Peace Plan; **103–104 Chris Bryant:** Chris Bryant, MP for Rhondda. Chris served as Deputy Leader of the House of Commons and Under-Secretary of State for Europe and Asia. He was also Shadow Secretary for Culture and Shadow Leader of the House of Commons; **110–111 Koen Schoenmakers:** Koen Schoenmakers is the Co-Founder and Chair of the Positive Impact Society Erasmus; **113 John Lydon:** Quoted by John Lydon; **114 Aristotle:** Quoted by Aristotle; **126–128 Juan Fernando Cristo:** Juan Fernando Cristo, Colombian lawyer and politician and ex-President of the Senate of Colombia. He was Interior Minister from 2014 to 2016, during the time of the peace negotiations with FARC and was one of the lead negotiators in those talks; **138 and 141–143 Gary Noesner:** Gary Noesner, FBI hostage negotiator. Gary spent 23 years as a hostage negotiator for the FBI and was Chief of their Crisis Negotiation Unit. He was technical consultant on the Netflix series, Waco, and was one of the main characters in the series. He developed the core hostage negotiation framework, The Behavioural Change Stairway, and wrote the best-selling book, *Stalling for Time: My Life as an FBI Hostage Negotiator*; **147 Napoleon Bonaparte:** Quoted by Napoleon; **148–150 Paul Chard:** Paul Chard, Chairman of Northampton Croquet Club, who found a creative way to resolve a local dispute; **159–161 Jo Hemmings:** Jo Hemmings, Behavioural Psychologist and expert Relationship Coach. Jo has been voted Dating Coach of the Year multiple times and has also sat on the panel. She is consultant psychologist on a number of television programmes and Assessment and Duty of Care Psychologist for several reality tv series. She is the author of several books on psychology and relationships; **177–179 Danny Russell:** Danny Russell, Brand Insights Consultant. Danny has spent 28 years building expertise in strategic insight for major global brands including 21st Century Fox, Vodafone, The Economist and Sky TV; **181 Deborah Tannen:** Quoted by Deborah Tannen; **193–194 David Villa-Clarke:** David Villa-Clarke, BEM, Founder of DVC Wealth Management. He is also Chairman of Project Volunteer, a charity supporting projects in Africa for the last 15 years, and CEO of the Aleto Foundation, a social mobility charity providing leadership education for young people from under-privileged communities. David was awarded the British Empire Medal for his commitment to charitable services and mentoring.

Pearson's Commitment to Diversity, Equity and Inclusion

Pearson is dedicated to creating bias-free content that reflects the diversity, depth and breadth of all learners' lived experiences. We embrace the many dimensions of diversity including, but not limited to, race, ethnicity, gender, sex, sexual orientation, socioeconomic status, ability, age and religious or political beliefs.

Education is a powerful force for equity and change in our world. It has the potential to deliver opportunities that improve lives and enable economic mobility. As we work with authors to create content for every product and service, we acknowledge our responsibility to demonstrate inclusivity and incorporate diverse scholarship so that everyone can achieve their potential through learning. As the world's leading learning company, we have a duty to help drive change and live up to our purpose to help more people create a better life for themselves and to create a better world.

Our ambition is to purposefully contribute to a world where:

- Everyone has an equitable and lifelong opportunity to succeed through learning.
- Our educational products and services are inclusive and represent the rich diversity of learners.
- Our educational content accurately reflects the histories and lived experiences of the learners we serve.
- Our educational content prompts deeper discussions with students and motivates them to expand their own learning and worldview.

We are also committed to providing products that are fully accessible to all learners. As per Pearson's guidelines for accessible educational Web media, we test and retest the capabilities of our products against the highest standards for every release, following the WCAG guidelines in developing new products for copyright year 2022 and beyond. You can learn more about Pearson's commitment to accessibility at:

https://www.pearson.com/us/accessibility.html

While we work hard to present unbiased, fully accessible content, we want to hear from you about any concerns or needs regarding this Pearson product so that we can investigate and address them.

- Please contact us with concerns about any potential bias at:

  https://www.pearson.com/report-bias.html

- For accessibility-related issues, such as using assistive technology with Pearson products, alternative text requests, or accessibility documentation, email the Pearson Disability Support team at:

  disability.support@pearson.com

Introduction

How do you change someone's mind?

In 2009, voters in Maine rejected legislature to allow same-sex marriage by 53 per cent to 47 per cent. In November 2012, those same voters changed their mind and this time the law was passed by the same margin of 53 per cent to 47 per cent. How did that happen?

Well, that's what this book is all about – persuading people to change their mind. And, moreover, does so in a way that wins friends, doesn't lose them.

Whether you're for same-sex marriage or against, you will want to change the mind of the person on the other side of the table. Whether you're Republican or Democrat, Labour or Tory, a Brexiteer or a Remainer, a vaxxer or an anti-vaxxer, if you're for Black Lives Matter or against, if you're for #MeToo or against, you will want to change the mind of the person on the other side of the table.

And, of course, it's not just politics – it's at work too. If you want that pay-rise you deserve, you will need to persuade your boss (and probably their boss and HR and the Finance Director too); if you want the client to buy your product, you need to persuade them it's worth their while; if you want the supplier to give you a good deal, that's persuasion; if you want to take a day off work in a busy period, persuasion too.

And if you want your lounge to be tidy, you need to persuade your kids to pick up their toys; if you want to go out with someone, you need to persuade them you're a great catch; if you want your partner to take Kevin as part of the divorce settlement and let you keep the dog, while they are arguing strongly for the opposite, it's all about persuasion.

Whether we are talking the boardroom or the bedroom, whether we are talking persuasion, influence or negotiation, it is all about changing minds. We even need to change our *own* mind at times: maybe it is about time I started saving a little money for when I'm older; maybe I should say sorry to my ex after all.

There are a lot of minds out there that need changing.

Persuasion isn't easy

Getting someone to change their mind isn't easy. If you've ever been on Facebook or Twitter, you'll know. Of all the political arguments you'll see there, you can scroll down as many pages as you like and never in the history of social media has anyone ever said, 'Oh yeah, you're right. I've changed my mind'.

Doesn't happen.

Why is this? Because we go about persuading the wrong way.

We persuade ourselves of the merits of our case and then assume the same argument will persuade the other person. We take it for granted they will see the situation exactly the same way we do.

But they don't and our argument lands on deaf ears and we're left with kids' toys all over the lounge, no pay-rise and friends who vote for the other party. Our world seems to be full of people who are either stupid or being deliberately difficult.

There is good news

In my day job, I run workshops on influencing and I often start by telling my delegates there is bad news and good news about the topic. The bad news is that there are nearly 8 billion people in the world and they are all different. So how on earth do you know how to persuade that given individual sitting in front of you?

The good news is that they tell you.

Of course they don't tell you explicitly, but all the time they leak the information you need to know – ask poker players. It is just a question of being able to tune into it.

So, shooting from the lip, going straight in with your suggestion or request, simply doesn't work. Instead, there is set-up work you need to do first and what would normally be seen as the persuasion process itself needs to come last.

Six steps to persuade anyone anytime

So, what is this set-up work? In this book, we're going to lay out six simple steps for you to successfully change anyone's mind.

1. Know what you want and aim high

If you are unclear about your outcome, you can't expect to get it. If you say, 'Guys, follow me' and they say, 'Yeah, where to?' and you reply 'Hmm, not sure, I'll get back to you', it's not going to work.

In a complex world, human beings are attracted to certainty, so the more you've thought your outcome through, the clearer you can communicate it and the more likely you will get it. In Chapter 1, we'll tell you how to do this and we'll encourage you to be ambitious. Great outcomes are out there to be had!

2. Do your preparation

Don't take the persuasion situation for granted. Just like anything of importance, we need to prepare.

You've got to know your stuff, know their stuff, know how your stuff impacts their stuff and brings them benefit. Know how they think, how they make their decisions, how they will feel.

In Chapter 2, we will show you the research you need to do before you make your request and this will massively improve your chances of success.

3. Become a world-class listener

Persuasion is ultimately built on listening, listening deeply, listening behind the words, listening between the words, listening for what is not said. And this is how we gather the information we need to be successful.

We all listen and we can all listen so much better. Quite simply the best listeners are the best influencers. Chapter 3 will tell you exactly what to do and exactly what you should be listening for.

4. Be strong, it will make them more collaborative

In Chapter 4, we will stress strength. Why? Is it so you can force your view through? No, not at all. We will argue a very ethical collaborative approach. We will argue that power should not be a factor at all.

However, sadly, in the reality of our species' current state of evolution, it does still need to be considered.

Put simply, it's amazing how collaborative the other person will be if you have a bigger army than them. So we will argue to build your strength, not so you use it but precisely so you don't have to use it.

5. Create the solution together

The solution does not exist with one person, it exists with you both.

You have a request, but they have a legitimate pushback. Or you have a solution but they prefer another. Or you have information that suggests one route forward but they have different information that suggests another.

There is an answer that will suit both people but you have to work together to find it. Chapter 5 will show exactly how to find the right solution that everyone can support.

6. Find the right way to put your message across

Lastly, Chapter 6 explains the best way to communicate your message – what will work for one person won't for another.

And the fact it is last does need to be stressed – very few people bother to go through the other steps first and this is exactly why they fail. To find the right words in Chapter 6, you have to do the pre-work in Chapters 1–5 first. But if you have done all that work beforehand, you will be surprised how smoothly it goes.

Multi-billion-dollar negotiations become nice conversations; airlines refund your cancelled flight; husbands volunteer to do the dishes. No, really.

Does this method actually work?

Let's go back to Maine in 2009. The LGBT community had a very clear idea of what they wanted: it was what the heterosexual community already had – that, all of that and no more than that. Equality, didn't seem like too much to ask.

But it didn't work, so they needed to find another approach. Now, they knew many people would never be persuaded and, equally, many were already on their side, so their job was to find those persuadable voters and find out what exactly would change their mind.

And that's what they did. Using focus groups and other market research methods, they spoke to 250,000 people who had voted against them but were most likely to change their minds. And they listened to what they had to say and began to get a better understanding of their views.

This is how they learnt why their original approach had failed and what they needed to do instead.

The 2009 campaign had been about demanding equal rights, and the demands were often put quite aggressively. But when they listened to these potential swing voters, they discovered that for them marriage wasn't about rights and equality at all – it was about love and commitment and family.

So they changed their modus operandi and launched a new website that captured this: www.whymarriagematters.org. If someone visited the homepage, the first words they saw were 'Love. Commitment. Family.' next to a picture of a heart and a home. Then, the question in big letters, 'Why Marriage?' followed by the answer, 'Because marriage says "We are family" in a way that no other word does'.

They had listened to the community and they were telling them they understood and agreed.

There was more. At the top of the page was a short video of four couples sharing their views on marriage. There was a black straight couple who had been married 31 years, a white straight couple, a lesbian couple and two men who were celebrating their 57th anniversary together the following month.

And the views? As schmaltzy and apple pie as you could get: ‘I would just say that love is love, it belongs to everybody’, and so on. Another video was of an elderly couple who went to their priest when their daughter came out; the priest’s advice was ‘She is the same person that you loved yesterday’.

You get the picture. This website was the basis for their new campaign which was all about *the values of the voters* rather than the demands of the LGBT community. Framing their message this way enabled them to achieve their goals. Three years after the first vote, there was a second – and this time they won.

The same campaign continued elsewhere until there were enough voters, state and federal judges, mayors, senators and even presidents on their side and finally on 26 June 2015 the Supreme Court decided that marriage was a fundamental right for same-sex couples across the country.

So it turns out you can change people’s minds.

And, in actual fact, in the book we’re going to look at professionals who work in the very toughest of situations. Not just persuading people who voted against LGBT rights to vote *for* them, which is hard enough in its own right, but we’re also going to look at hostage negotiators, interrogators and forensic interviewers, and counsellors who work with addicts and repeat offenders. These are extreme cases.

And, interestingly, we will see that each of these fields independently developed remarkably similar methods that prove successful even in such extreme circumstances.

But aren't we being manipulative?

Do no harm.

Influencing is something we do all the time: when I ask you to pass me the salt, I am influencing your behaviour. So, as with everything, do it to the best of your ability, do it the way that works. I'm a believer in using good persuasion methods for ethical ends: if you are persuading them to do the right thing, the good thing, then persuade them as well as you possibly can.

But it is true that influencing is a tool and, as such, is inherently neutral but can be used towards good ends or bad. And you can bet the bad guys are going to use the best practice, so why shouldn't the good guys?

But how can we be sure we aren't being manipulative? How does it differ from:

- A tobacco advert creating a need in you that you didn't have before, a need based on a lie of the beautiful lifestyle in the advert?
- A political party framing a self-serving policy in terms of helping the poor?
- A website luring you towards a purchase you don't really need?

Dictionary definitions of manipulation usually include influencing to your advantage (with no reference to the other person's advantage), often without the other person knowing and often dishonestly.

So a good starting point is intention. If your intention is for the best for the other person, then we are on the right track. But who is to judge? Maybe, in his own mind, Hitler felt he had good intentions? This by itself is not enough, it is just too easy to fool ourselves. We need to check our methods more diligently.

7 WAYS TO ENSURE BETTER ETHICS

1. Be open with your intention.
2. Make it about their benefit as much as yours.
3. Don't cheat, lie, misrepresent or hide any ulterior motive.
4. Work together for a solution everyone is happy with.
5. Allow them freedom to say no.
6. At all times communicate based on respect and unconditional positive regard.
7. Only use methods you would be happy for someone to use on you.

The more of these we tick, the more comfortable we can feel our methods are fair and not manipulative. And if it ever becomes complicated, refer to the following:

Do no harm.

The really good news

My mother is Irish Catholic and my dad was English Protestant. I grew up in the 1970s and every time there was a bomb in Northern Ireland (or, for that matter, the mainland), the civil war was fought at our dining table.

Even at the age of 10, I thought there must be a better way.

I'm writing this book because there is. A better way to solve political disputes than throwing bombs and killing people and a better way to resolve differences of opinions in the family than shouting and name-calling.

This is the really good news. The approach outlined in this book is going to get you much better results in your life and get you much better relationships. And, more than that, one conversation at a time, it will make the world a better place.

So let's do it.

Aim high

1.1 Aim high

Ok, put the book down and go off and find a paperclip. That paperclip is the key to your future riches.

Great. Found one? Your instruction is to now trade that paperclip for a house. Reckon you can do it?

Kyle MacDonald of Vancouver did. It took him 14 trades over the period of one year but he got there. And managed to write a book, *One Red Paperclip*,[1] about it as he went.

He traded:

1. The paperclip for a fish pen
2. The fish pen for a doorknob
3. A doorknob for a stove
4. A stove for a generator
5. A generator for an instant party
6. An instant party for a snowmobile
7. The snowmobile for a trip to Yahk, British Columbia
8. A trip to Yahk for a van

9. The van for a recording contract
10. The recording contract for one-year free accommodation in Phoenix
11. The year in Phoenix for an afternoon with Alice Cooper
12. An afternoon with Alice Cooper for a motorised KISS snow globe
13. The snow globe for a movie role
14. The movie role for a house.

This man aimed high and well done to him for doing so.

1.2 Know what you want, what you really really want

If you want to change someone's mind, it's important to know what you want to change it to.

- If you ask your teenage son to tidy the lounge, don't be surprised if they do *their* version of tidy which might be very different to yours. You have to be specific about what exactly you mean by tidy.
- If you ask for a pay-rise, don't be surprised if they give much less than you had in mind. You have to communicate clearly how much you want.
- If you pay your artistic friend to create a sculpture for your hallway, don't be surprised if their vision of beauty is different to yours and you let out an involuntary yelp when it's unveiled.

So, the first step of the process is to be very clear about the outcome you want. The more you have thought that through, the more accurately you can communicate it and the more likely you will get it.

Why do we want it?

Knowing why we want it is important too. As Mick Jagger once told us, we can't always get we want – hey, that's the world we live in – but if we know why it is we want it, we might be able to find another way to achieve it.

My mother is 90 years old and she lives in a care home. During the coronavirus pandemic, I tried to visit her but the nursing staff wouldn't let me. Why? Because they didn't want to risk me introducing the virus into the home and causing a devastating outbreak. Why did I want to see my mum? Well, *she's my mum*! I wanted to see if she was ok. I wanted to check if she needed anything. I wanted to show her we hadn't forgotten about her. I wanted to hug her, of course, but I knew that wouldn't be possible.

So the solution? They brought her out to the reception and sat her down by the window and I was able to talk to her from outside. No chance of transmitting the virus through glass and me and Mum could chat.

Asking the question 'Why?' gets around the roadblocks.

Why? Why? Why? Why? Why?

In strategy, they recommend asking the question 'Why?' five times because this gets you in touch with what's really important to you.

Kyle MacDonald wanted the fish pen because he knew it would help him get something else which would help him get something else. . . which would help him get a house.

Let's take another example. You are trying to persuade yourself to go to the gym but you've had a long day at work and the sofa is calling. Why do you want to go to the gym? Clearly to get fitter. So why do you want to get fitter? Well, you say, to get more energy in your life. And why more energy in your life? So you can play with the kids more. Why do you want to play with the kids more? Well, this is what you love doing most of all, the kids *are* your life.

Brilliant, now you've reconnected with your most powerful motivation and now you'll find it so much easier to say sayonara sofa as you run off to the gym.

Why is where it's at

When you think about what you want and then ask why you want that, it puts you in touch with an even more important goal than your first answer and this kind of thinking will bring you greater success. People who get fixated on that first-level goal are not always successful; people who focus on the reasons behind the goal are.

This is because the question why gives much more flexibility. Often there are very good reasons why your request cannot be met, so focusing on those reasons and the reasons behind your own request will allow a lot more room for a solution.

If you see a lovely jacket in a shop and you find out it costs £200 but you only have £100, you are unlikely to get it and no amount of negotiation or pleading or bursting into tears will change that. If you are stuck on that jacket at that price, you're going to be disappointed.

But why do you want it so much? Well, you need something to keep you warm as winter is coming, and the styling is beautiful, you will look so nice in it and it is a really funky shop. Fine, if that's what you're really after, you can probably find a nice jumper in the same shop that you can wear with your existing jacket – the jumper ticks all the boxes and is within your budget. We got our result.

TOP TIP

Whenever you have a choice between the easy option and the 'right' one (e.g., sofa or gym), remind yourself why the right one is right. Ask that question 'Why?' as many times as you need to make the right choice.

Lining up your goals

Human beings have evolved a lot of goal-seeking neurology – whether it's to produce food and shelter or to get the latest Porsche. Our ancestors who were best able to get what was needed for survival were clearly more likely to survive. So, defining our goals in this manner triggers that wiring, which helps us achieve them – noticing opportunities, solving problems, identifying routes, energising and so on.

And it can be really powerful to line up your outcomes so that achieving one takes you nearer to getting the next, bigger one.

Kyle MacDonald's Why Five Times answer was he wanted a house. If he had entered an estate agency and tried to buy one with his paperclip, they would have laughed him straight back on to the street. But he was able to be flexible and each trade took him closer to that house.

John D. Rockefeller was the world's richest man at the turn of the twentieth century and one of the richest ever in inflation-adjusted figures. Hardly surprising given his company, Standard Oil, largely monopolised the oil sector.

But he didn't build the monopoly directly, he always knew that if he took the direct approach there would be too much resistance. So he took a different route. He secretly bought all the freight companies that transported the oil and this gave him a stranglehold on the industry. This was a much better strategy.

Now I think about it I'm disappointed MacDonald stopped at the house. He should have aimed to corner the oil market.

TOP TIP

Work backwards from the long-term goal. Let's say the goal is world domination in five years, ask where will you need to be in four years' time in order to achieve it. And therefore where will you need to be in three years' time, and so on, until you get to the present.

What's your favourite birthmark?

Anne Nusselder, Opfrisdame – Freshen-Up Girl! The Opfrisdamen bring improvised theatre to festivals, corporate functions and care homes for the elderly. Anne teaches (visual) storytelling and presentation at the University of Arts, Utrecht.

'I do what I call intimate acting, 1-to-1 acting. No, it's not what you're thinking. I'm paid to interact with people at an event of some kind and freshen up their minds. And I do this mostly by really paying them attention. I ask a lot of questions, we get close, they get moved or they get surprised, but they definitely get Freshened Up.

Now I do like to bring a bit of fun to it and a few years back, I happened to be using the children's game with the folded paper – the one you move with your fingers and thumbs and fold back the paper and there's a question written underneath. I approached a woman who was about 60 years old and who looked a little quiet but she was up for the game and the question she got was: "What's your favourite birthmark?"

Interesting question and I got an interesting response: "One on the right cheek of a man's backside!" Who would have expected that from this demure little lady?

I pressed: Was it a specific backside that she knew or one she was looking for? One she was looking for. Wow, she was looking for something special!

I put her on the spot: Have you ever asked anyone if they had such a birthmark? No, of course not, she was mortified at the thought.

Now this was a crowded event and I looked around and saw a lot of men and one great big opportunity. I stood on a chair and asked very loudly if there were any guys in the vicinity with a birthmark on their right cheek.

Lo and behold, someone stepped forward, indeed a good-looking man about the same age as the woman, as

➤

> it happened. I did the only thing I could do – I made the introduction then left them to themselves.
>
> The happy ending? I received an email from the lady a few months later to say she had found the birthmark she was looking for and the two of them were now a couple.'

1.3 You have to ask

What a lovely story. But, of course, the sad implication is that the woman took 60 years before she found her birthmark. All because she was too shy to ask. And what if she had never met a Freshen-Up girl who had the guts to make the request for her?

And how many people live their lives without getting what they want because they don't think or are too frightened to ask? Each one a tragedy.

You have to ask.

That seems so elementary and yet so frequently people forget or are afraid. Of course, asking does not mean you will receive. But you can be quite sure that not asking means you will not receive.

Your life or your parking spot

And it's the big things like love and it's the small things too. Many years ago, another friend of mine, Diana, moved into a beautiful flat in central London. We're talking really central, a lane off a lane that ran between Leicester Square and Trafalgar Square.

Beautiful flat, fantastic location, one problem: there was no parking and she had a gorgeous pink convertible Peugeot 504 that was the love of her life. What to do?

Well, she had a brainwave. There was a hotel on the same street that had underground parking and she thought she could only ask. As it happened, her grandfather had been the agent who brokered selling the plot of land on which the hotel was built. Doesn't have the same pulling power as being the owner's daughter (if you're reading, Ms Hilton) but it was worth a try.

Unfortunately, the try didn't work. She told her story and made her request but the management weren't able to help. Oh well.

Except, about two months later she received an email from the hotel to say that one of the staff parking spots had become vacant and if she was still interested. . .

She was still interested.

4 WAYS TO GET THAT CHEEKY ASK

1. Be friendly first, show interest in them.
2. Ask with a smile.
3. Give them a (vaguely) plausible reason to say 'yes'.
4. Thank them even if they say no.

1.4 Don't discount yourself

Far too often we aim low instead of high. Here's a typical scene:

{Night before}	Tomorrow I'm going to walk into my boss's office and demand a pay-rise. I've done my market research and I know I deserve at least 10 per cent, probably a lot more but I'll settle for absolutely nothing less.
{Next morning}	Well, they'll get angry if I ask for 10 per cent, I'll ask for 9 per cent. Well, 8 per cent, just in case.
{In boss's office}	Hi boss, I've done some market research and I can prove that I deserve a 7 per cent pay-rise. But, er, I'd be happy to accept 6 per cent. *{Boss scowls}* Ok, I'd be happy to accept 5 per cent.
{Boss replies}	We could give you 2 per cent.
{You}	4?
{Boss}	2.5.
{You}	Ok.

You negotiated a quarter of what you were worth, of what you could have got had you taken a different approach.

But it's worse than this because if that's how you negotiated this time, you'll do the same the next. And the next. And the next. If you only ever negotiate a quarter of the annual pay-rise you deserve, at the end of a 40-year career you will be earning only slightly more than one-fifteenth of what you should have been.

And that will apply to everything else in your life too. Sounds pretty depressing, doesn't it! *Now* are you going to ask for what you deserve?

And don't forget, psychologically speaking, if you discount yourself, you are telling the other person you are worth less. If you need a brain surgeon, you don't go to the cheapest, you go to the best. But you can't do sufficiently rigorous comparisons to evaluate who's best, and price is actually a reasonable indicator, so there is a tendency to choose the one that is, as Stella Artois claim, reassuringly expensive.

In a world where value is difficult to calculate, people take their cue from the figure you give them. We often assess the value of a product or service by its price. So, charge low and they won't think you're any good; charge high and they will.

TOP TIP

Write down your figure and you will discount yourself less. If the meeting is on the phone, have it on a big piece of paper on your desk so you can always see it; if it is face-to-face, write it in your notebook and have the notebook open.

I stopped being afraid they'd say 'no'

Vitas Poshkus, founder of PVA Developments, a design-orientated construction company specialising in bespoke residential projects for private clients.

'When I started my business as a builder, I priced myself really low because I was desperate to get every single job that I could.

I wasted so much time putting energy into dealing with difficult clients – they were always complaining, always asking for discounts, always asking for extra things. It was a nightmare and I could never grow the business like that.

But with time I began to believe in myself that the value I brought the clients was worth what I was charging. I stopped seeing myself as a muddy-boots labourer but rather as a company director; I started wearing a shirt and jacket and I bought a Lexus instead of my old van, and the clients began to have more confidence in me.

I bought a really nice watch for my birthday once and shortly after I went to see a client and he made a nice comment on it. After the job, he told me he knew I was going to do the work for him as soon as he saw the watch. It was an indicator of quality for him.

I stopped stressing about losing the work. Now I love those first meetings. I enjoy bringing my expertise and showing how I can help them. I look around and I find something I can connect to and start a conversation about, maybe they have a cat and I'll tell them about my own cat. Now I have much better relationships with my clients, it's much more human.

And with all of this I stopped giving a muddy-boots price and instead I gave a company director price. Sure, it meant I lost some work, clients who wanted a muddy-boots labourer, and that was the hardest thing for me to do.

But mostly they were happy to pay because they knew they were going to get a Lexus job on their house rather than an old van job. Plus it meant I could give more time to my existing clients and do a better job for them and that was a much better strategy.

In 2012, I employed 10 people and was pricing £20–30,000 for a job. A year later it was 40 and I was pricing at £80–100,000 and clients were happy. By 2018, I had 140 staff on my books and I was working on jobs worth well over a million. I learnt to stop being afraid clients would say "no".'

1.5 Aim high, aim really high

I'm just saying, don't undersell yourself. Kyle MacDonald achieved an extraordinary outcome but maybe those extraordinary outcomes are out there more than we imagine.

Back in the late 2000s, I ran a strategy workshop for one of the large consultancy firms, working at global 'Head of' level. I set them a brainstorming task and gave them an instruction to generate as many ideas as they could, including at least two 'impossible' ones.

Now, these were very pragmatic people and they didn't really like the brainstorming exercise but they joined in the spirit and they came back with a couple of ideas that made them laugh with how ridiculous they were.

The first was: 'We're going to get rid of all our staff and then we won't have to pay any salaries and our margins will go through the roof'. They giggled as they said it. Until I pointed out that Wikipedia, one of the largest brands in the world had about 30 employees at the time. A few years later, when Instagram were bought by Facebook for $1 billion in 2012, they had just 13 employees. The impossible idea had already been done.

'Ok', they said, 'our second idea is really impossible. We're going to invent a mind-reading machine that will read the minds of our clients and so we can give them what they want before they even ask for it'. Hilarious, they thought. Until I pointed out that Google Ads effectively did exactly this and their impossible idea had turned Google from loss-making to one of the largest and most profitable companies in the world.

Two impossible ideas that had not only already been done but had made their organisation incredibly successful.

We need ambitious thinking. We are an amazing species and we can create many amazing things but there is still a huge amount of poverty in the world, there are still huge disparities in power, there are huge inequalities in education, the potential catastrophes of global warming and environmental destruction loom large and wars and famines still destroy the lives of millions.

Nelson Mandela didn't compromise his thinking when he changed the minds of the apartheid regime in South Africa. Those behind the Good Friday Agreement didn't hold back when they brought an end to the Troubles in Northern Ireland.

We need ambitious thinking more than ever.

TOP TIP

Always think of at least one impossible idea; it just might lead to a possible one.

1.6 And in the kitchen?

Ok, ok, I understand, many of you are thinking you don't want to become a tech billionaire and you don't want world peace (well, you do but that isn't why you bought this book), you just want your husband to get off the sofa and do the washing up.

I get it. Family database Uinvue found that an average family spends 91 hours a year arguing – that's nearly four full days – and the most common reason is who's doing the household chores.[2] Personally, I think we should argue for the whole of the first four days of January and then we've got it over and done with for the year.

But the same principle applies, you see. Why limit your thinking to something simple like that when, if you go about it the right way, you may get so much more? You may even be able to get your husband to clean the whole house; maybe even get him to *like* doing it so you never have to ask again.

So, after deciding what you want and then asking why (five times, of course), ask another question: what would be an amazing outcome?

It is just worth considering.

On a recent workshop, a delegate mentioned they had a meeting the next day with their landlord who wanted to increase the rent. The delegate's outcome from the meeting was for the rent to stay the same. But when we asked what would be an amazing outcome, it occurred that they might even be able to *decrease* the rent.

They knew the landlord was very busy and didn't like the hassle of the role – fixing things around the house, organising new tenants and so on – so if they offered to take on some of these jobs, that would surely be worth a rent reduction. After all, agent's charge 15–20 per cent. A good friend of mine lived for decades in the same luxury apartment with next to no rent rise on exactly this basis.

Extra-ordinary outcomes are out there, even in the kitchen, think extra-ordinarily and you can achieve them. I'm not promising you will always get them. But you just might and you certainly wouldn't if you didn't do the thinking.

Now it's worth remembering that family harmony probably sits somewhere among your Why Five Times answers, so while you might be very keen to change your uncle's crazy political views, is it really worth ruining the Christmas dinner over? Or causing a huge family rift? Probably not. Beyond a certain point, a live and let live approach is often wise if you value a happy family or you want to keep your friends as friends.

I had a choice: succeed or die

Igor Rybakov, serial entrepreneur, venture capitalist, philanthropist, on the list of the world's richest people according to Forbes. He is co-founder of the Technonikol corporation, and founder of the Rybakov Foundation and the Rybakov Prize (called by Forbes the 'Nobel Prize in Education') and the X10 Academy, a school for entrepreneurs.

When I interviewed Mr Rybakov he told me that in 2003, his company Technonikol, the largest roofing company in Russia, the company he had spent years building up, faced an existential challenge. The market was changing and customers were demanding more modern insulating materials, and unless he could offer them this they would simply go elsewhere.

So he approached Rockwool, the global leader in mineral insulation, and made an offer to buy 15% of all the global capacity of new factories they built from that time onwards, which he felt was a generous offer.

But Rockwell would have none of it and laughed when he suggested he would build his own factories. They said it was impossible, that he may be an expert in roofing but he knew nothing about mineral insulation, they were totally different technologies.

This was like a red flag to a bull for Mr Rybakov so he decided to burn his bridges with Rockwool and he went to the market. But there simply wasn't anything there of the same quality which meant he now faced a stark choice between building high-quality factories himself or watch Technonikol die.

There was one tiny possibility: to find a producer of the previous generation technology and convince them to make latest generation machines, developing the technology as they went, but no one was willing to take such a huge risk.

But eventually he found one person, Mirko, a Slovenian engineer with a background from a German engineering school, but even Mirko thought it impossible. They spent a long time discussing it, how they might create 'the new Russian Rockwool' and finally Rybakov asked, 'If you don't believe in the idea, could you believe in me?' There was a moment, then Mirko said 'Igor, I will support you.'

They signed the first contract on a napkin.

They made the announcement to Mirko's team (who also thought it impossible) and they got down to work. A year later, the production line produced its first mineral insulation, in one-third of the time normally required to build such a plant. They all celebrated that they had managed to achieve so quickly something that all the experts had said was impossible.

Within four years, they built seven more production lines, with Rockwool looking on, not believing what they were seeing. Rybakov admitted Rockwool had been right, it was a massively complicated technology, but they went from zero competence to market leaders within the space of a year.

As of today, Technonikol is the market leader by a long way in the ex-Soviet territories and they are number two in the world. They matched Rockwool in their own field. And Mirko has become one of the strongest and most successful suppliers of technology in this market.

These days, Mr Rybakov runs the X10 Academy, where he helps entrepreneurs achieve goals many times bigger than they thought possible. 'I teach people', he says, 'to create teams where there is no need to persuade. For me persuading or convincing someone is almost a form of force.'

With Mirko and everyone else who thought it impossible, 'I didn't persuade them; instead, and much better, I inspired them and they trusted me.' He calls it a 'social blockchain of trust' – where people trust each other so much that there is no longer a need to convince or persuade.

'If you can find "your people", everything will succeed. Not just for you but for all of them too.' If you can do this, he believes, 'you becomes us, yourself becomes ourself' and this is when the magic starts.

He says it creates an excitement and it's the excitement you need to build roads, bridges, hospitals, ships, it's the excitement that transforms people and brings about extraordinary results.

With Mirko and with his other projects and with the X10 Academy, Rybakov has a community of people who are sure they will succeed. They are attuned to a great future, they are convinced that something good will happen.

'And', he says, 'it *does* happen.'

1.7 Aim high for both parties

I appreciate that up to this point I've been exhorting you to aim high, but you're probably thinking 'All well and good, Simon, but when I ask for my 10,000,000 per cent pay-rise, my boss is going to tell me to go back to my desk and carry on with my work and be thankful for what I get'. Having the ambitious outcome is one thing, but persuading someone to give me it is another.

And, to be fair, so far I have only given you a few ideas that can help in that persuasion process. Don't worry, by the time you've finished the book you will have dozens more, but here is one that will go a long way: aim high for them too.

This is counter to the old-school negotiation approach which deems it best to haggle them down as far as you can. But nothing is going to lose their sympathy quicker than being greedy and nothing is going to trigger their defensiveness quicker than taking something at their expense.

Let's go back to the pay-rise. Often our justification is to do with our new house/child/lifestyle/addiction, and this just won't cut it. If we're a little smarter, we give a *business* case: how we consistently went beyond our objectives and exceeded our targets. But, usually, the boss knows they have already banked this and so they don't care. But if, instead, you connect your rise with something they do care about, perhaps something that will help them achieve *their* targets or earn *them* a pay-rise, well now they're listening.

If I'm a lawyer and I give an estimate to my client for £10,000, they might say it is beyond their budget and no amount of haggling will change their mind. But if I show how my advice will save them £20,000, they will find that budget.

Igor Rybakov got a 'no' everywhere he looked. But when he was able to show how much success he would create for everybody else, people came on board.

So, don't be like the Neanderthal negotiator who tries to win at the other person's expense. I say the opposite, aim high for them as well as yourself.

Help them get *more than they thought possible themselves*.

1.8 Aim for the moon and hit the sun

In 1992, Alex Ferguson, the manager of Manchester United FC, set his sights on buying Alan Shearer to help the team win the English league for the first time since 1967. Shearer was the best centre-forward in the country and consequently the most expensive and he sold for a record £3.6 million – to Blackburn Rovers.

Ferguson aimed high; he tried to get the best, but it didn't work out. A few months later, though, he received a phone call from Leeds United managing director Bill Fotherby. While they were talking, Ferguson asked if Eric Cantona would be available. Fotherby said he would get back.

An hour later, Cantona was sold to Manchester United for £1.2 million. Cantona brought the skill but, more importantly, the mentality that the team needed and they went on to win the league four out of the next five years.

Ferguson didn't get Shearer but he did get Cantona and it kick-started his incredible run when he won 13 out of the next 21 Premier League titles.

So even if you don't get your aim-high outcome, you might get something else that you would not have got otherwise. And that something may even be better than you had originally wished.

When do-do happens, what do you do-do?

Of course, sometimes things go wrong, sometimes really wrong; it is part of the journey.

In June 2014, Amazon launched to great acclaim a huge new product, the Fire Phone, that was going to be their route into dominating the mobile phone market.

It sold well for two weeks and then figures dropped rapidly. Four months later, Jeff Bezos announced they had lost $170 million on the project and sales had trickled almost to a halt.

Unmitigated disaster. Except. . .

. . . Bezos had seen an early prototype and was knocked back by its speech-recognition capabilities. Within days he had set up a whole new department to focus on this and, exactly as the Fire Phone died, Alexa was born from its very ashes.

Alexa has been sold on well over 100 million devices.

So things can appear to go wrong, but that is not the end of the game.

TOP TIP

If you have a big setback, just re-calibrate. Where is it you want to get to? Where are you now? Right, what do you need to do? Then get on and do it. Pretty soon you'll be back in the groove and you'll achieve your goal.

Life isn't a one-shot game

Your request might get a 'no', but don't give up.

In 1997, in Santa Cruz, a small company was launched with a big idea of delivering movies to every house in the world. There was a problem: a typical film took months to download with the technology of the day so their first model was to send DVDs in the post. Not really the great solution they were looking for.

But they knew it wouldn't always be this way and they held on to their vision. The company was Netflix and their founder Reed Hastings said, 'When we first started raising money, we thought we'd be mostly streaming in 5 years. In 2002, we had no streaming'.

Hmm, this plan is not going well, let's tweak it a little. 'So we thought that by 2007, it would be half our business. In 2007, we were still nowhere'. Where's that plan?!

As of 2021, it is streaming to over 200 million households.

Just because you don't reach your goal at first request, doesn't mean you will never get it. These things aren't one shot and one shot only. As Geoff Mulgan said about his time in the Blair government, 'We always over-estimated what we could do in the short-term, but we always under-estimated what we could do in the long-term'.

Failure isn't final. Life isn't a one-shot game.

I like to imagine the first attempts at space flight by billionaires Bezos, Musk and Branson involved jumping.

3 QUESTIONS TO ACHIEVE MASTERY

After each attempt at your goal or each try to change someone's mind, whether you were successful or not, ask yourself these three questions:

1. What worked?
2. What didn't work?
3. What could you do differently next time?

This is the process of continuous improvement; this is the process of mastery. Do it every time and you will achieve great goals and become a master at changing people's minds!

In summary

When we try to change someone's mind, we typically dive straight in with our suggestions without thinking it through. This is a formula for failure.

Instead:

- Know what it is you want

  If you think it through and be very clear about your outcome, it will be easier for you to communicate and the more likely you will achieve it.

- Know why it is you want it

  This will give you much more flexibility in terms of achieving your goal. Sometimes we can't get exactly what we want, but if we know why we want it, we can find the way to achieve that bigger picture objective.

- You have to ask

  Don't ask, don't get; ask, and you just might. Don't waste your life wishing for something when you may have got it had you just asked.

- Don't undersell yourself

  Too often we discount ourselves even before we ask. We have to value ourselves because if we don't, how can we expect the other person to?

- Aim high, for you *and* the other person

  Be ambitious, go on! Successful people don't spend their life wondering if they could have got a better outcome – they give it a try. And be ambitious *for them too*. Help them get more than they thought possible themselves. If you can do this, they will now be helping you achieve your ambitious goal and so you will be more likely to get it.

- Life is not a one-shot game

  What if you don't get your outcome? Don't worry, keep trying until you do. And maybe your efforts will get you something different, maybe something better.

Great, now we know what we want, but we're still not ready to persuade. All it means is we have persuaded ourself. If we want to change someone else's mind, we need to do a bit of research into how we might best go about it.

Look for clues

The people hacker

Jenny Radcliffe, social engineer, human factor security expert, people hacker. Jenny uses her expertise in non-verbal communication, deception and persuasion techniques for ethical white hat hacking to help secure client sites and protect them from malicious attacks. She was part of the special operations unit for the successful Channel 4 series 'Hunted'.

'I'm a hacker, but I'm not the stereotypical hacker in a hoodie behind a computer, I'm a security consultant and I work with psychology, as a "people hacker". My job involves physical infiltration, when organisations or high net worth individuals give me permission to try and bypass their security measures and gain access to their premises.

These are necessary exercises to expose security flaws and educate clients, so that they can fix the gaps and the bad guys can't come along and do the same thing as me. So, I'm an ethical hacker; consider me a burglar for good.

One client asked if I could try and gain access to his office inside a building on what he considered to be a secure site. He said, "You'll never get in. We've just spent £2m on the

➤

perimeter defences, we've got fences, alarms and guards. The only way you'll get in is if someone leaves the door open for you, and that will never happen."

Accessing any site requires detailed planning. I use open-source intelligence techniques (OSINT) to research the industry, the organisation, the building and the people. I'm looking to find any levers or triggers that they will respond to, that might be exploited. This is often something that fits in with their values and beliefs or with the way they operate and conduct their business.

My research showed that this company was traditional and hierarchical, operating in an industry with multiple safety considerations. It was important people followed rules and this was a key part of their company culture. The management were "god" and people did what they were told. So that's what I worked with.

To breach the fence, we used a pellet gun to shoot a crack in a car windscreen and then posed as a car maintenance and repair firm, as per the staff benefit package. This convinced their security staff who let us through the fence, but we still needed to get into the building. My "windscreen repair" colleagues left and I hid and waited.

I had prepared a piece of paper, with "Please do not close this door. Thank you." printed on it. I'd signed it with a vague signature, and printed "HR Dept" underneath. It looked official enough and I sellotaped it to the currently closed, external fire door.

After a while someone came out and paused as they saw the sign on the door. Then they obediently wedged open the door and left.

I waited, watching people leave, each happily leaving the door open as per the sign telling them to do so. After most people had left for the night, I walked through the door into

> the factory and found the client's office. I took some pictures to prove access and left my calling card for him to find in the morning, and that was the infiltration complete.
>
> If I had been a criminal, the consequences of this type of security breach would have been very serious.
>
> They were only eight words, but used in the right place with the right person, it worked.
>
> It wouldn't have worked at every site; it might not have worked on a more casual company or in a rebellious culture where rules were not seen as so important. However, used in the right place with the right people, that piece of paper was able to open the door.
>
> Eight words, but if you know how a group of people operate, then sometimes that's all you need. Psychology and culture do the rest.'

2.1 The secret to making persuasion easy

So we've learnt to aim high and we've learnt if we don't ask, we don't get. But that doesn't mean if you ask you will always get. Sometimes persuasion can be really difficult. Sometimes it is beyond the other person's control to grant your request – 'I would love to help you, but my hands are tied'.

But there are always answers, if we look hard enough.

Over the years I've been teaching negotiation skills I've worked with many top negotiators. One colleague who was regularly involved in nine-figure deals in London's financial Square Mile described his negotiations. 'It's strange', he said, 'I will go to the meeting, I'll shake hands with the other person, we have a nice chat over a cup of coffee and then we sign the deal and then I leave. It's not like a negotiation at all, it's just a nice conversation'.

How come? Was he just such an amazing negotiator? Natural born? Or lucky?

No, none of those. It was just that he had done the preparation. That meeting was at the end of days, weeks or months of preparation.

If you want the conversation to go really smoothly, the secret is in the preparation. Do that research and you will find the clues you need to persuade.

What should you prepare? Lots! Almost every paragraph of this book is an item to cover in your preparation. Know the facts, know the figures – yours, theirs, the competitors, the benchmarks. Things won't necessarily go in a straight line so scenario plan, know the what-if's, anticipate the difficult questions, the push-backs, the offers and your responses to all. Do the thinking now, so you don't have to do it later, under pressure, in the conversation.

TOP TIP

The ABCD of research is Always Be Collecting Data and this is a good guideline to remember. Look for clues everywhere and you will find them and they will help you in your mission.

And prepare your mood. You probably find that when you're in the *right* mood, you're unstoppable, so what can you do beforehand to make sure you're in that mood in the meeting? What mood does it need to be? Super-confident? Strong and robust? Quick-thinking and alert? Charming? Whatever it is you need for your conversation, do what you need to do to get in that state of mind and then the results will just follow.

Now I know some people can be afraid of these situations, but it doesn't have to be like this. Even the toughest of conversations can seem like a nice chat if you prepare properly. You can enjoy them; you can even look forward to them.

And if you do, you will almost certainly get better results.

2.2 Clues in the context

In your research, you will find clues – clues everywhere; clues that can help you change their minds.

You will find clues in the context. We can learn a lot about someone from the context. Where do they work? Where do they live? Do they spend their time in the gym or the pub? Do they spend their money primarily in Harrods or at the Saturday car boot sale? If you're meeting in a restaurant of their choice, are they taking you to the local McDonald's or for some posh nosh in Mayfair?

In fact, some studies have shown that the location actually impacts personality profiling scores. For example, people tend to measure higher on extraversion in cafes, lower on neuroticism in places of worship and higher on conscientiousness in gyms.[1]

So, expect a different response accordingly. Expect a different response if you are meeting at a wedding or at an academic conference. Expect a different response if there is an economic crisis going on or a time of plenty.

It turns out that people make their decisions partly depending on the context – wow, who knew? Well, maybe you did, but did you know just how *much* it depended on context? And how you could, therefore, use it?

It can be really nuanced. Researchers put four bottles of French wine and four bottles of German wine on sale in the wine section of a supermarket: on days that French music played in the background, three times as much French wine was bought than German; on days German music played the figures were reversed. And when asked about their choice, 86 per cent of shoppers said specifically they were not influenced at all by the music.[2]

Context counts. You can learn much from it and you can strategise how you might persuade better.

Try speaking in a French accent, you never know.

2.3 Clues in their story

A few years ago, I had a sales meeting with a large law firm and I did some quick research on the person I was meeting. My usual strategy for a law firm is to play it straight – smart suit and tie, nice briefcase and polished shoes.

But five minutes on Facebook showed me this person happened to be the lead singer of a thrash metal band. I took a different approach to normal.

Human beings are just human beings. So if you're trying to persuade someone, bear that humanity in mind.

One of the most successful negotiations in recent times was the Northern Ireland Good Friday Agreement which ended decades of civil war in the region. The process was chaired by Senator George Mitchell and anyone who wanted to get something into the final agreement would, ultimately, have to persuade him.

In the three years of the negotiations, Mitchell married, had a baby miscarried, another one born and his brother died.[3] So many emotional moments of such intensity, these were bound to be on his mind, no matter how professional or heroic he tried to be. Taking this into consideration could make or break your request.

Understand their perspective

But it is not only such high stakes negotiations or such life-and-death events. In any situation one thing you can guarantee is that the other person will see the situation very differently to how you see it. And, typically, we have our rationale, our evidence to back that up and we think 'It's obvious, isn't it?'

But they have a very different perspective, they have a very different rationale, they have their own evidence to back that up and they think '*That's* obvious, isn't it?'

And what we do is go back to our rationale, louder. And it doesn't work.

And this is why our world is full of irrational people making crazy choices. Actually, they're not irrational, it's just they have a different rationale to ours.

What we need to do, instead, is take the time to step into their shoes, understand their perspective and then put our outcome in terms of their rationale. That's the only way that will work. Anything else and they will say 'Yeah, but you don't get it'.

One of us

If we know someone's story, we know who they are and this is crucial if we want to change their mind. If they see us as different to who they are, if we are a 'Them' to their 'Us', it will be very difficult to persuade.

Human beings are very tribal – for good reason: for millions of years the animals we feared the most have been other human beings. So, we have deep wiring to distinguish between 'Us' (safe, can trust) and 'Them' (definitely not safe, definitely can't trust).

Mark Levine and his colleagues at Lancaster University conducted a great study where they invited a group of Manchester United fans in to write an essay (a bit ambitious, I thought) about why they were a Manchester United fan.[4] It was then set up that as they left the building, they saw a runner slip and obviously hurt themselves. If that runner wore a Manchester United shirt, 92 per cent of people went over to help; if they wore a Liverpool shirt, only 30 per cent helped.

The really interesting part of the experiment was the second phase where they invited a similar group of United fans to come in and write an essay, but this time the essay was about why they were a football fan. Now, 80 per cent helped the Liverpool fan. It was no longer 'I'm a Manchester United fan, they're a Liverpool fan', it was 'I'm a football fan, they're a football fan'.

We are all plural. I'm a man, a middle-aged man, yes Stale Pale Male! I'm English, I'm half-Irish, I'm Essex Man, a West Ham fan, a football fan. I'm an author, I'm a trainer, I'm an occasional meditator, I'm an avid reader, I'm an ex-trapeze artist, I'm a scuba diver. I've travelled to 80 countries; the likelihood is I've visited your country and if I did, I almost certainly loved your country. I'm a son, I'm a brother, I'm a human being, and so much more. . . we have a quasi-infinite range of identities and they all have different perspectives and attributes and at any given point in the day I might be in one and at the next moment I will be in another.

This is good news. It gives us the opportunity to find that overlap with the other person, through knowing their story. And once you have done this, you can build a deeper connection with them and work with them so much more effectively.

8 WAYS TO BECOME 'ONE OF US'

1. You work in the same field.
2. You live in the same town.
3. You have the same interests or hobbies.
4. You have had a similar experience in the past.
5. You are from the same background.
6. You are the same age.
7. You are the same gender.
8. You live on the same planet.

2.4 Clues in their personality

If you want to change their mind it helps, of course, if you know how they think – and there are all kinds of personality tools that can help with this.

Some like Myers–Briggs and DISC are used a lot in the office; Belbin is used for the team context; and others ('Which kind of squirrel are you?') don't seem to have much use at all.

One that is very relevant to changing minds was developed by Doctors Kenneth Thomas and Ralph Kilmann and is known as the Thomas–Kilmann Instrument which categorises people according to how they manage conflict. Unfortunately, Thomas and Kilmann fell out when deciding on the name. . . ok, no they didn't, just my little joke.

They identified five different types of people.

1. Competing

The competer likes to fight, looks for a fight. They want to win and they want you to lose.

Thomas: I *insist* we call this the Thomas–Kilmann Instrument.

2. Accommodating

These are the 'nice' people, too nice, people who lose out.

Thomas: Let's call it the Kilmann–Thomas Instrument.

Kilmann: Oh no! We'll call it the Thomas–Kilmann Instrument, that's much better.

3. Avoiding

These are the scaredy-cats, the people who don't like conflict at all.

Thomas: What shall we call our fantastic new instrument?

Kilmann: Erm, good question, can we talk about it later?

4. Compromising

The 'split the difference' types who think compromise is win–win (when in actual fact it is lose–lose; neither side fully gets what they want).

Thomas: Shall we call it Thomas–Kilmann or Kilmann–Thomas?

Kilmann: How about Kiltho–Masmann?

5. Collaborative

The sensible, intelligent, successful type, usually good-looking, who work together to find a solution that suits everyone.

Thomas: We can call this model the Thomas–Kilmann Instrument. . .

Kilmann: . . . and we'll call the next one the Kilmann–Thomas Instrument.

(*High fives*)

Let's hope Kilmann especially isn't the competitive type because he might sue me for defamation of character, but I am confident he is the sensible, intelligent, successful, good-looking, collaborative type so I should be ok.

Joking apart, the TKI can be a really useful exercise before any negotiation or persuasion situation. It will help predict the other person's likely response and which approach would be your best option.

Each of the types has got their place but, as you've probably guessed already, this book suggests the collaborative approach will be most successful in the large majority of cases.

The OCEAN Big Five

In recent years, the scientific world has coalesced around the OCEAN Big Five tool as the profiling instrument of choice. I suspect there is an element of self-fulfilling prophecy here – it seemed to be studied more than the others, which gave it more credibility, and so it was studied more, which gave it yet more credibility – and so on.

Whatever its history, the net result is that it is the tool with the most amount of credible research to back it up and therefore the most rigorous scientific support. This model also identifies five types of people, but these types are applicable to a much wider context than just conflict.

Once you know what type they are, you can tailor your message accordingly. In 2012, Hirsh, Kang and Bodenhausen published a study that showed how you might do this.[5] Their experiment presented five different advertisements for a fictitious 'XPhone', each targeting one of the traits. Respondents were much more likely to judge the advert effective if it matched their dominant personality style.

These are the Big Five personality types, their characteristics and the XPhone advert most effective.

1. Openness

   Openness to new ideas: those who score high on this dimension are typically creative, curious, tolerant, politically liberal; a low score on this scale correlates with pragmatic, down-to-earth, politically conservative.

   'With the new XPhone, you'll have access to information like never before, so your mind stays active and inspired. . . '

2. Conscientiousness

   People high on this score are typically organised, focused on the goal and work hard; those low on this score are often more spontaneous and easy-going.

   'With the new XPhone, you'll never miss an important message, simplifying your work life. . . '

3. Extraversion

   As the name suggests, people high on this score are sociable, friendly and often loud; those who score low are more reserved, serious and likely to prefer time on their own.

   'With the new XPhone, you'll always be where the excitement is. . . '

4. Agreeableness

   Friendly, trusting, co-operative people score highly on this dimension; assertive, self-orientated, people who disagree a lot with others score low.

   'With the new XPhone, you'll have access to your loved ones like never before. . . '

5. Neuroticism

   High scores here suggest an anxious, self-conscious worrier; low scores suggest a calm, self-confident and stable type.

   'Designed to keep you safe and sound, the XPhone helps reduce the anxiety and uncertainty of modern life. . . '

TOP TIP

Don't depend too heavily on the label. Just because someone is normally, say, extraverted doesn't mean that they can't enjoy time by themselves.

Use the right nudge with the right person

Patrick Fagan, behavioural scientist, visiting lecturer at three London universities, the author of 'Hooked: Why cute sells. . . and other marketing magic that we just can't resist' *(Pearson). Previously Lead Psychologist at Cambridge Analytica, he is currently Chief Scientific Officer at behavioural science consultancy Capuchin.*

'I'm a behavioural scientist and my job is to use psychology to influence people in the real world.

For example, I've recently completed a study where we used targeted nudges to increase the likelihood that people would save a phone number for a suicide prevention helpline into their phones.

In the first phase we had nearly 500 people complete an online survey, starting with a questionnaire that enabled us to psychologically profile them with respect to various demographic factors like the OCEAN Big Five tool, their gender and their age. It also profiled them with respect to their persuasion profile, using Cialdini's six influencing principles. Then at the end of the questionnaire, there was a request to save a crisis line number into their phone.

Now each group had a slightly different message. The first group had a very neutral message but the second one conformed to Cialdini's "Authority" concept (that people are more likely to be influenced by the trappings of authority) and the third to his idea of "Social Proof" (that people are more likely to be influenced if others are doing the same). For the authority nudge, we told them that experts say it works and gave them statistics to back it up, using high-credibility language. For the social proof nudge, the message stressed how other people are using the number, that it was a popular thing to do and so on.

And then we measured how many people saved the number to their phone. And what we found out was that these nudges worked. Both the authority and the social proof nudges increased the likelihood of saving the number by about 14 per cent.

But when we looked deeper and saw how the nudges worked with specific personality types, we got even better results. For example, women who scored highly for being conscientious were especially influenced by the social proof message. In fact, they were 40 per cent more likely to save the number compared to the same nudge used on other people.

So we followed this up with a second phase, where we specifically allocated a social proof message to women who scored highly on conscientiousness and randomly split everyone else to either the same social proof nudge or to no nudge at all.

From our control group, random population with no nudge, 14 per cent saved the number into their phones. From the random population with the nudge, 29 per cent of people saved the number, more than double. But a full 50 per cent of the conscientious women receiving the nudge saved the number.

So, these nudges work but they work even more effectively if we use the right nudge with the right person.'

2.5 Clues in the wider picture

If we want to understand the other person's perspective, we need to understand the world in which they live. This world will involve many people: their family, their friends, their boss, their boss's granny's dog and so on. Ok, the boss's granny's dog doesn't officially count as people, even if it thinks it does, but you understand my point.

- If you want to persuade your child to go to the extra homework classes, it might improve your chances of success if you ring up the parents of their best friend first and check if they are going too.
- If you are trying to persuade your neighbour to trim their tree but they are slow in getting round to it, a friendly letter from the local council saying the bye-laws allow you to trim it yourself (with you suggesting a date you're free), might be the thing that nudges their elbow.

So widen out the picture and answer the questions: 'Who else is involved?', 'Who else can be involved?' and 'Who else do you need to get involved?'.

Let's put this in a corporate context and we can use the model developed by Bourne and Walker,[6] a model they called The Seven Directions, to identify key stakeholders:

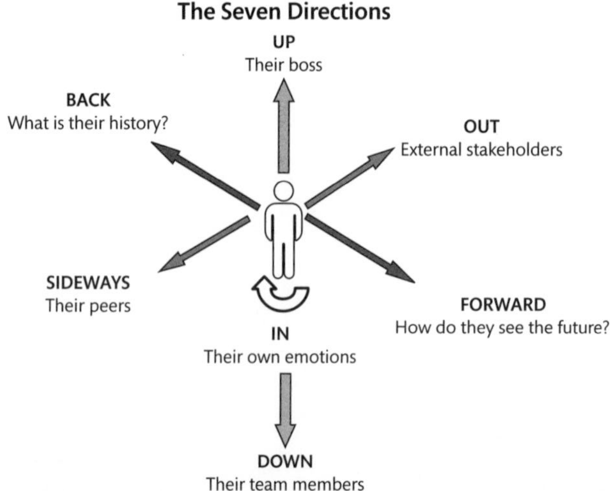

For you to understand the other person's perspective, you need to know what's going on with their boss, with their team members, with their peers and so on. And the more you know this, the more successfully you will persuade.

You can apply your own variation of this model even outside of work. Take a sheet of paper and draw on it everyone involved. You don't have to be a great artist, I can't even draw stick-people and it still works for me, but the visual mapping can provide a deep understanding of the situation. Somewhere on that map you will see someone (or someone's dog) that is the critical person (or dog). And that's how you will get your answer.

TOP TIP

Use as much visual richness as you can. Drawings, different colours, different types of lines or shapes can all carry extra information and bring a better understanding of the situation.

When Yanis Varoufakis became the Greek Finance Minister in the middle of his country's debt crisis, his job was to persuade the famous Troika (the European Central Bank, the European Commission and the IMF) to buy into his plans for re-structuring the debt. But for this he needed to get more support from the political leaders of Britain, France and Germany.

Hardest of those to persuade would be the British government, famous for their love of austerity. If they were putting their own country through such tough measures, it was a slim chance they would allow any other country to get off lightly.

But Varoufakis had an unlikely ally. Three years earlier at an event in Australia he had met Norman Lamont, a grandee of the Conservative party and an ex-finance minister himself, and they had become very good friends. A quick call to Lamont and then a call from Lamont to George Osborne, the British Finance Minister, and the meeting was a surprising success.

And not a dog to be seen.

Understand the power dynamics through visual mapping

Dr Lynda Bourne, stakeholder engagement expert, lecturer at Monash University and Director of Professional Development at Mosaic Project Services. She is a recognised international authority on stakeholder management and visualisation technologies, publishing papers in many academic and professional journals on the topic.

'I advised a global port management company who built new container ports and updated existing facilities in partnership with other organisations around the world. The work in each location was very similar, but for success the company really needed to understand the nature of the local stakeholder relationships and these would vary hugely.

Each specific location would have its own complex web of organisations including port management authorities, national government agencies, other shipping lines and operators and even local populations, and the attitudes and relative importance of each needed to be understood. And, of course, each partner organisation would have very different reporting structures, very different decision-making processes, very different national cultures – all of which needed to be understood thoroughly if the partnership were to be successful.

So the approach they took was a detailed stakeholder identification process based on teams using the "directions". Mapping this enabled them to get a solid grasp of the diverse power relationships and the communication processes needed to influence decisions and move each project forward.

The situation was made even more complex by the fact that the same organisation may be collaborating in one country and competing in another. In these instances, they used the analysis to help manage the relationship and communicate the information needed to work together but at the same time ensuring competitive information was withheld.

Using a disciplined and consistent process to the stakeholder analysis across all of the locations, they were able to achieve a better understanding of the stakeholder group at each port and the local power dynamics, and were therefore able to build more effective working relationships and more successful projects.'

2.6 Clues in the culture

In the globalised world of today, we can easily find ourselves trying to persuade someone from the other side of the planet; and if we want to do this, it helps if we understand their culture. Working with someone from Beijing is very different to working with someone from Paris, which is very different to working with someone from Mexico City and so on.

And if we get it wrong, it can be disrespectful and might break the whole deal. Many billions of dollars have been lost by organisations that did not take this factor seriously enough.

Clearly, there are too many cultures in the world to cover them all here, but it is worth your while learning some general principles.

7 WAYS TO WORK SUCCESSFULLY ACROSS CULTURES

1. Understand their culture as well as you can. Study it in every way possible.
2. Spend lots of time in their country.
3. If you don't know it well, find someone who does.
4. Compare your culture with theirs and note the differences.
5. Discuss any differences with the other person. Celebrate them.
6. Expect miscommunication and allow for it.
7. Meet face-to-face in your country or theirs if you can.

Of course, cultural differences aren't just national, they arise across regions within countries too – Milanese have a different mind-set to Napoletanos; New Yorkers are different to Texans; highlanders to lowlanders; coastal people to continental.

And it's not even just geographical: different industries will have different cultures, different organisations within an industry, different departments within an organisation, different teams within the department. There are cultural differences across age, gender, race, schooling, income strata, social tribe.

And then, for all your learning of their culture, remember that the individual is not their culture. So always treat everyone as unique. Use the cultural guidelines as exactly that – a guideline; but be ready to learn that this individual is quite different to their group's norm.

Ultimately, all interactions are cross-cultural; we are all in a culture with a population of one.

If you hold the pen, you have the advantage

David Landsman, former positions include British Ambassador to Greece, British Ambassador to Albania, Managing Director of Tata Ltd (Europe) and Director of UK India Business Council. An international negotiator and expert in corporate strategy and geopolitics, he is currently Chairman of Cerebra Global Strategy and Chairman of the British-Serbian Chamber of Commerce.

'As a former diplomat who previously studied linguistics, I've always been interested in the role language plays in diplomacy, in its broadest sense. Knowing the other person's language is of immense value. When I was posted abroad, I was almost always fortunate enough to have had the chance to learn the language before arriving, which without a doubt gave me an advantage over diplomatic colleagues who didn't.

Of course, you can hire a translator, but they can never explain every detail of how it's been said, the tone of voice or the implication. On the other hand, I've negotiated in the EU, NATO and the UN and I definitely don't speak everyone's language!

In the early 2000s, I was part of the European team negotiating with Iran on its nuclear programme. I had the advantage that the negotiation was in English, but it would definitely have been better if I had been able to understand Farsi too. As I recall, only one of our team did, whereas several Iranians understood English, which gave them many advantages: a few seconds' extra thinking time while the interpreter explained; they could pick up nuances better; and they could even understand the asides when we were talking "privately" to each other.

Even better is to be a native speaker of the language the negotiation's being conducted in – and today that's usually English. I recall one negotiation in the (then) G8 taking place in London under a British Presidency. We were trying to find a way of bridging a serious underlying difference about a recent development with North Korea and its nuclear weapons.

Some wanted to take a stronger line than others: some wanted to express "deep concern", others didn't want to go beyond "concern". We batted this about for a bit with no progress. Then I suggested we try an alternative: how about "profound"? Nods all round.

If you hold the pen, you have the advantage.

"Language" can go beyond whether you speak French or Farsi. It's important to think holistically about what's being said and when, by whom, as well as what's not said.

I was in Libya negotiating with senior members of the Gaddafi regime following his decision to abandon his chemical and nuclear weapons programmes. This was a difficult decision for Libya and the negotiations were tense.

The two lead Libyan negotiators were chalk and cheese, though both were very senior and had strong links to the Leader. One dominated the talks, spoke only in Arabic, often loudly and aggressively, and did a pretty good job of tiring out some of our team. His colleague, however, kept silent for much of the long negotiating sessions, although he spoke excellent English and no doubt picked up all the nuance. In the end, it was he who summed up calmly in a few words. No doubt who was boss.

Negotiators ideally speak the language(s) of the negotiation. If they're lucky, they hold the pen. But even if neither of these is possible, paying active attention to "language" in its broadest sense will certainly help.'

2.7 Clues in the channel

What's your favourite medium? Not who's your favourite psychic, but how do you like to communicate?

Everyone has their favourite channel, and if you want to change the other person's mind it is worth thinking about which channel will be best. A large part of the answer will be the channel *they* like best, whether that's face-to-face or TikTok or messenger pigeon.

We can learn a lot about them from their preference. If it's face-to-face, do they want a formal meeting at the office or would they rather a quick chat at the local coffee shop or the taster menu at a Michelin-starred restaurant? If it's video-conference, do they have the camera on or off? Do they prefer the phone or the latest still-in-exclusive-invite-only-mode platform?

We can learn about them from their communication style too. Many years ago, I was running two different projects with two different friends, both called Alex. One was hard-nosed investment banker Alex and the other was soft, fluffy, hippy Alex. Hard-nosed investment banker Alex would ring and the call would never last more than three minutes. It would be bish-bash-bosh and bye, no time for how are you. Soft, fluffy, hippy Alex would call and it would take an hour and a half whatever it is we were talking about. Before we talked about anything to do with the project, he wanted to know how I was feeling and then he would tell me how he was feeling and then he wanted to know how I was feeling about how he was feeling and so on.

I'm exaggerating, of course, and both Alex's were very good friends and both projects were successful projects, but I did have to bear in mind each other's communication style if I wanted to get my outcome.

Even if it's good old vanilla email there's a lot we can work with. Some people write long emails, some write one-word grunts, some don't even respond at all. Some are bullet-pointed, some start with asking about your weekend and others have lots of emojis and fluffy bunny rabbits.

It's all useful information about who they are and how you can best communicate with them to get your outcome.

In summary

If you want the conversation to go well, you can't beat doing the preparation. It's the same with everything – the results you get are a function of how well you prepare. And if you do that research, you will find clues everywhere to know how to persuade them.

- Understand their perspective

  One thing you can guarantee is they will see it differently to how you see it. You have to put your message or your outcome in terms of how *they* see it. Otherwise, it just won't get through.

- Become 'one of us'

  Human beings are tribal animals and you want to show that you and they are of the same tribe. This is not to fake it; you should be able to find a genuine overlap between who they are as a person and yourself. Once you've done this, they will be much more open to your idea.

- Know their personality type

  Everybody is different but personality profiling can be a quick way to understanding how someone thinks. If you know how they think, you can use this to predict how they are likely to respond to your request and how you might change your approach for greater success.

- Understand who else is involved

  It is never just you and that one other person, there are always other people involved – even if you aren't aware of who they are. But if you can map out everyone involved and identify their drivers, it can help you navigate a route through to success.

- Understand their culture

  Ultimately, everyone is in a culture of one, but understanding the person's broader culture in which they live and work can give clues as to how they might respond.

- Which channel should you use?

  Typically, we default to our favourite, whether that's email, phone or the rooftop restaurant with great views across the city. You might, however, want to choose *their* favourite channel instead. Either way, knowing their choice of channel and how they use it can give interesting pointers to how you can influence them.

So, look for clues everywhere. You have to listen for clues too, but we'll cover that in the next chapter.

3 Listen, listen, listen

3.1 An end to conversational narcissism

It's not all about you

This is perhaps the most important section in the book.

Most people view conversation as an opportunity to talk about themselves. I had a friend who I used to see regularly and she spent the whole time telling me of her latest woes. I put up with it until once when I was going through a difficult period myself. In the space of a month, I left my job, my father died, I broke up with my girlfriend and then found out she was pregnant. When my talkative friend heard this, she said, 'Oh wow, we have to meet up and talk'.

What she meant was, we have to meet up and talk *about her*. As we sat down at the café, I said 'How's things?' in an off-hand way, as you do, and she spent the next 90 minutes telling me all about how terrible her life was.

She's a friend I used to see regularly.

She's not alone. Many people love the sound of their own voice and their favourite topic is themselves. At their most gracious, they say, 'I've been talking way too long, your turn, what do *you* think, what do you think about me?'.

Charles Derber, in *The Pursuit of Attention*,[1] makes the distinction between the Shift Response and the Support Response and he recommends we do more of the latter.

In the Shift Response, we move the topic from them to us:

Friend: I've just come back from a great holiday.

Us: Oh me too. I went to Magaluf, it was brilliant, I went to this great bar. . .

At this point, our Friend is unlikely to feel especially friendly towards us. But if we chose the Support Response we would keep the focus on them:

Friend: I've just come back from a great holiday.

Us: Oh wow, where did you go?

Friend: I was in Magaluf for a week.

Us: Fabulous, what did you get up to?

Here, our Friend will feel more friendly.

It can be subtle. Sometimes, we want to add to their topic (Support Response), but we are so focused on what we are going to say that we stop listening to them. We simply don't have the room in our brain to hear them and our own thoughts at the same time.

TOP TIP

Sharing things from your own life is ok but make sure you finish by putting the spotlight back on them.

> 'I went to Magaluf too! Tell me, what did you get up to?'

The fact of the matter is that if you want to change their mind, you will need them to listen to you. But how can you expect them to listen to you, if you never listen to them? You can't.

If you want them to listen to you, you need to go first and listen to them.

The amygdala, an important piece of brainery

Amygdalum is Latin for almond and there are two small almond-shaped areas of the brain, called the amygdala, that play a tremendously important role in keeping you alive. Not only that; they played a tremendously important part in keeping your ancestors alive, all the way back through our evolutionary tree, all the way back to the duck.

Actually, we didn't evolve from ducks, but you get what I mean.

The amygdala is the part of the brain that deals with danger. If a bear were to jump out from behind a tree, your amygdala would instantly be alerted and trigger your fight or flight or freeze response before you could say, 'Oh look, there's a bear'.*

It is also the part that triggers aggression – the fight response – and the part that, when it thinks it is being attacked or under stress, dampens down many other parts of the brain so it can focus single-handedly on saving your skin.

One part of the brain the amygdala disrupts is the prefrontal cortex (PFC) – a part of the brain heavily involved in listening. The PFC receives information from the auditory cortex as well as other sites in the brain and puts all of it together for the purpose of rational thinking and making decisions.

* Not including koala bears

In other words, if you want the other person to hear you properly and fully understand what you are trying to say, and if you want them to be able to think rationally and make a good decision, you want their PFC to be fully mobilised, which means their amygdala needs to be quiet.

In other words, they must feel totally safe.

Interestingly, some studies have shown that challenges to our deeply held beliefs trigger the amygdala, exactly the same as a physical threat.[2]

Love and fear

> *'There are only two emotions: love and fear. All positive emotions come from love, all negative emotions from fear. From love flows happiness, contentment, peace, and joy. From fear comes anger, hate, anxiety and guilt. It's true that there are only two primary emotions, love and fear. But it's more accurate to say that there is only love or fear, for we cannot feel these two emotions together, at exactly the same time. They're opposites. If we're in fear, we are not in a place of love. When we're in a place of love, we cannot be in a place of fear. . . There is no neutrality in this.'*

This is a quote from Elisabeth Kübler-Ross, the Swiss-American psychiatrist, named by *Time* magazine as one of the top 100 thinkers of the twentieth century.

What she is saying is that if we don't want the other person to be in a place of fear (and thereby trigger the amygdala and shut down their ability to listen and process), they need to be in a place of love.

Now, as above with listening, if you want them to be in a place of love, you need to go first and be in a place of love too.

For some of you, this is going to be an extraordinarily powerful learning and you will put the book down and go out into the world full of love and transform the results you get. That difficult neighbour, that annoying colleague, will become your best friend.

Others will be muttering about love and hippies and how it all went wrong in the 1960s and what on earth has this got to do with persuading the security guard to let me through even though I've forgotten my badge.

To be fair, love is quite a strong word here, so let us talk about affective primacy doctrine instead.[3] Affect, quite simply, is whether we are drawn towards something or pushed away. In the same way that an amoeba moves towards or away from certain conditions that it detects, our brain, fundamentally, processes huge amounts of information from the outside world and does the same. It decides whether we should go towards it (nutrients, supportive conditions, reproduction) or away from it (harsh conditions, pathogens, predators). We're really not that dissimilar to the amoeba.

And it makes this decision to approach or avoid in a tenth of a second. A tenth of a second.

Affective primacy doctrine says this comes first and impacts all subsequent brain processing, including reasoning. That is, if we like something (positive affect), we will come up with reasons to support it; if we don't like it (negative affect), we will come up with reasons against it. The reasoning is a post-hoc rationalisation of the affect.

For example, we judge good-looking people to be smarter than average and they are more likely to be acquitted by juries; our evaluation and reasoning are a result of the positive affect we have for them.

In other words, if we think love is too strong a word, we still want them to have positive affect towards us if we want them to change their mind.

Unconditional positive regard

According to Dr Will Schutz, the inventor of FIRO theory (Fundamental Interpersonal Relations Orientation), all people:

- want to feel significant and are afraid of being ignored
- want to feel competent and are afraid of being humiliated
- want to feel likeable and are afraid of being rejected.

This lies behind so much human behaviour so perhaps your simplest way to change anyone's mind is to show them that, to you, they are significant, they are competent, they are liked.

Along similar lines, Carl Rogers introduced the idea of unconditional positive regard. Rogers, inventor of humanistic psychology and considered by many to be one of the most eminent clinical psychologists of the twentieth century, believed that therapeutic change can only occur if there is unconditional positive regard – a genuine caring for them, not contingent on any specific behaviour.

All of these approaches – love, positive affect, unconditional positive regard and helping them feel significant, competent and liked – are ultimately just different flavours of the same dish, they are all saying the same thing.

Why, if they don't deserve it?

Now, you may be thinking the person you are trying to persuade doesn't deserve this: their behaviour has been too far out of order. Maybe they're an alcoholic and it's caused too many problems; maybe they're a gambler and they have lost too much of the family's money; maybe their political opinions are anathema.

Well, remember in Chapter 1 we said know your outcome then *always* stay focused on it? So, let's check. Has what you've been doing to date worked?

With the alcoholic and the gambler, has the nagging worked? Has telling them what a waste of space they are worked? With your political foe, has your irrefutable logic and splendid set of supporting evidence ever persuaded them of the error of their ways? Unlikely. So, to achieve your outcome you will need to try something different.

Why hasn't your approach to date worked? Probably because you haven't addressed this element of their need for psychological safety, so they shut down and don't hear anything you are saying and they certainly don't change their mind.

But let's see what happens when you do address this need. In 2012, Google launched Project Aristotle, a multi-year study of performance across all the teams within the organisation in order to identify which teams were the most successful and what were the key factors that lay behind that success. They found that the biggest factor by far was psychological safety.[4]

So, for purely pragmatic reasons it's worth a try: this could be the thing that will work for you. It has a great track record working with exactly such difficult cases as alcoholics, gamblers, indeed addicts of any kind. It works in the hardest of cases, it works with criminals, with repeat offenders, with police interrogations, with terrorism interrogations.

A genuine caring for them, for a suspected terrorist? Why would you do this? For the simple reason that it works. For the purely practical purpose of getting your outcome.

And ultimately that *is* what you want.

Whether you call it love or positive affect or unconditional positive regard or lowering the excitation levels of the amygdala, if it gets you your result, it's worth doing.

And the simplest way we can achieve all this is through listening, really listening.

I got my Dad back

Aliya[*] *is a barrister and works as an in-house legal counsel for an investment bank.*

'I was born and bred in Hertfordshire but I'm from a Bangladeshi background and I found myself leading two lives – in my daily life I was the Western me, the true me, but at home I respected the boundaries and was a good Bangladeshi daughter. It wasn't always easy.

When I was at uni, I met a guy, a Pakistani guy, who I liked and we started seeing each other but it didn't go down well with my dad. Many of my dad's friends had died in the Pakistan/Bangladesh war and now here was his golden child wanting to go out with the "enemy"!

We had a big argument and it was the first time I ever challenged him: his war wasn't my war. More than that, he had to understand I had grown up in a different way to him and he just couldn't expect me to be like him, I needed to choose my own way of life.

But he stopped talking to me and, in turn, I started avoiding him. I would make sure I never had dinner at the same time with him: I wouldn't eat at all or I would wait until everyone had gone to bed and then sneak in and make some food.

This went on for a couple of months, but eventually I decided to do something different. I loved my dad and that was the relationship I wanted with him.

So I decided to stop avoiding him and one evening I sat at the table again as normal. He didn't say anything but that was ok, I just wanted to be there with him.

For the first few times, I didn't say anything; I just brought a positive energy. Then I started to join him and Mum watching tv in the living room, but he still wasn't talking to me.

* Aliya is not her real name

Then it was around the time of my brother's wedding and everyone was getting excited and we needed a new gate for the front of the house. I suggested this to Mum and she said "Oh why don't you go down to B&Q with your dad and get one?". I looked at him and said, "Shall we?" and he agreed. And we were at the checkout and the gate dropped on to my foot and Dad instantly reacted. "Oh my God!", he shouted and leapt forward to stop it landing on me. He was really worried I'd hurt myself and I was fine but, you know what, it was the first caring thing he had said to me for ages.

It was a breakthrough; I was delighted. He showed me the care and love that I had been looking for, that I knew all along that he felt, and I was so happy that he was able to express it.

I knew his intentions had always been good. He wanted the best for me and he thought he knew what that was. But I needed to show him that ultimately I was going to make my own choices for my life and I could make good decisions. But I also needed to do that in the most loving way that I could.

After this, we got back to normal, in fact we became closer than ever. We spoke a lot more. There were a lot more loving conversations, trying to understand each other. I told him more about my life, the mixed environment I'm in, and he was really receptive and interested in it.

I hadn't told him before because I was afraid he would be angry but perhaps if I had been more open with him earlier, he wouldn't have been so shocked when he found out about the boyfriend.

I sometimes think that if none of us had any resistance, we'd be overflowing with love for each other. But we're too fearful, too self-protective. That's what happened with me and Dad: there was a breakdown, through misunderstandings and miscommunication, but ultimately there was always lots of love.

In the end, I made a stand for that love. It took perseverance, but I persisted. And I got love back in return. I got my Dad back.'

3.2 Listen to understand, not refute

Look, even if you don't buy into that yucky love or positive affect stuff and even if you can't tell your amygdala from your elbow and don't want to, there're lots of other reasons why you should focus on listening if you want to change the other person's mind.

Mind you, listening is difficult. We've got other things on our mind, there are distractions, we're planning tonight's dinner, the other person doesn't help by talking in a monotone voice. We haven't even evolved to listen well, we've evolved for our attention to jump around, scanning the world for danger: Is there a predator ahead or behind us? Is there a shark in those bushes or a tiger hiding behind the curtains? Staying focused on one specific channel for an extended period of time goes against our wiring.

So how do we listen well?

The most important thing is your intention. If you get your intention right, what you need to do will follow. And even if your listening is clumsy, you will be forgiven as long as your intention is clear.

So what should that intention be? Well, as above, the most powerful intention is based on love. And I appreciate this is difficult at times, when that person who nearly ran you over is now swearing obscenities about your mother out of the window. However, the more you can get to that place, the better outcome you will get.

If it helps, love them for selfish reasons, love them simply because it works.

At the very least, your purpose should be to understand. This is not the norm. In an argument, we typically listen to refute. We wait for something they say that we can pounce on with a rebuttal. And they do the same to us and the argument gets nowhere.

You can see this in social media. You see 'Yeah but. . .' comments all the way down and zero success rate in changing minds.

But if you are open about your intention, that you are trying to understand or help, and if the conversation gets difficult, you re-share that intention – they will be much more likely to open up.

After intention comes attention

All forms of listening involve full attention. Mentally decide that you're not going to think about anything else: not about your to-do list, not about your next meeting. Stop multi-tasking, put the phone down, switch off the tv and look at them. Sitting alongside, or at a slight angle, is often better positioning than directly opposite because there is less pressure on the speaker and it creates more of a sense of 'us'.

As you're listening, do what hostage negotiators call 'minimal encouragers' – those unobtrusive behaviours that show you are listening. People have a deep need to feel listened to, so it is not enough to listen: the other person needs to feel fully listened to. Short words like 'Yes', 'Ok', 'I see', 'Got it', 'Uh-uh' and nods of the head will help.

Allow silence: silence is thinking time. Some people have to do their thinking by talking it through, so allow them that space.

Reflect back some of the things they say. This can be a simple repetition of a couple of key words or it could be a larger summarising.

TOP TIP

Play back their argument better than they could have done it themselves. Then, and only then, make your proposition.

And as you listen, try to go deeper and connect some dots. You aren't just taking it in, you are processing too. What must be true for them to say that? What are its implications? How does it fit with other things they've said? What is going on for them to say what they're saying? How would I be thinking/feeling/behaving if my world were such that I said this? More importantly, given what else I know about them (and dropping what I know about me), how must *they* be thinking/feeling/behaving in this situation?

And at the same time, do none of this but just sit there being with them in their experience. Processing gets in the way of listening. So how much of one and how much of the other should you do? It depends on the outcome. The Samaritans would say just be there with them; but if you need to understand a complicated argument, you might need to be more active in your questioning. Finding that skilful balance of active or passive engagement at the right time for each comes with time.

And, with any processing you do, remember it's a guess. If you joined three dots to make a triangle, maybe that triangle only exists in your mind and not in the real world. There's only one way to find out – ask! 'One thing that comes across to me is. . . ' or 'I'm getting a sense that. . . '. And then they can tell you whether you're right or not.

She had to change her mind before she could change his

Sue Atkins, The Parenting Coach. Sue is the Parenting Expert on ITV's This Morning *programme as well as BBC Radio, Disney Junior,* Good Morning Britain *and a host of other shows on television across the world. She has been a Parenting Coach for over 15 years.*

'When parents come to me and ask for help with their child, very often it's the mind-set of the parents that I need to change and only then can they change the mind-set of their child.

It's quite common for parents to be taking an overly directive approach that isn't getting them the result they are looking for and that's why they have to come to me. Constantly telling, and not listening, sends very negative messages to children, regardless of their age, and they're just building walls not bridges between them. If the child feels pushed, they will push back.

So, when I'm working with parents, I will tell them stories about my own children and other families I've worked with, and help and guide them to understand some different approaches to parenting.

Recently, I had a couple come to see me about their teenage son, Mike, who was on the computer too much. Mum's attitude was quite aggressive, and she was threatening to take Mike's computer away for the next 6 months! Dad thought she was a bit on the dramatic side, but that wasn't helping their parenting because it just made them argue.

So, I sat and listened to their story. I was curious about the situation and asked lots of questions. I was non-judgemental, relaxed and shared some amusing anecdotes; nothing too patronising. But I connected with them, and I created an environment where they could feel safe, enabling them to move to that same way of communicating themselves.

Often parents find this difficult at home, because they're too close to the situation: when they're in the middle of what I call 'the socks and pants of life' they can't see the bigger picture. So, they often just wind each other up and end up in an argument; but working with me, both parents felt it was a safe space to explore their differing points of view. Both sides could listen to each other more and both sides could then feel heard, as I act as a sounding board.

I often ask them to bring a photo of their child. I remember a Zoom coaching session with a couple who were divorcing, and I asked them to put a picture of their daughter, Ruby, on the screen as we worked together. During the session the father said something that was inflammatory, and the mother responded, and it looked like another argument was about to start. I just said, very calmly, "What would Ruby think of that?" He looked at the picture of the child, and said, "Oh my god, it's a terrible idea". It was the reminder of the very real impact on the daughter that made him realise he needed to change and rethink his approach.

So, back to Mike's parents, I used another strategy. I put a piece of paper on the floor and I asked Mum to stand on it and, as she did so, I asked her to step into the shoes of Mike and tell me what he was feeling. There was an immediate shift. "Mum's really annoying, she keeps nagging me. . . I just want to do the same things as my friends. . . otherwise it's boring. . . Mum and Dad are arguing. . . there is a lot of tension in the house. . . ." It all came out and for the first time she really appreciated how her son was feeling.

Dad did the same and then I encouraged them to talk with each other and they listened, in a way they clearly weren't doing at home. And this made all the difference.

Now, her concern had been that Mike was spending his life playing computer games and this wasn't healthy for him, as it was unproductive. But when they got home, they all talked it through as a family and looked for answers that would be good for everyone. It came out that Mike liked running and he also decided to take up boxing. These were healthy activities that he enjoyed, and Mum approved of, which meant she felt she could be more relaxed about the computer, and it was agreed he could spend an hour a day on it.

She had to change her mind before she could change his.'

3.3 Listen with your ears

In my introduction, I said people tell you how to influence them – you just have to listen. But what do you listen for?

- You listen for their drivers: what is it that they want and don't want, their hopes and their fears. Because if you can put your message in terms of those, they will be more likely to agree.

  If you want your husband to mow the lawn and you know he wants to watch the football later, you could suggest, 'How about you mow the lawn this afternoon, then I'll cook a nice dinner while you watch the football later?' You're linking your request to their drivers.

- You listen for other emotions: emotions are indicators of their responses to situations and stimuli so if you understand their emotions, it will help you predict their likely response to your proposition. From this you can tailor your proposition accordingly and they will be more likely to agree.

- You listen for their criteria: the specific attributes they are looking for in their goal. For example, they tell you they want to eat out this evening and they think they have communicated clearly. But what do they actually mean? You could suggest McDonald's and be off by a mile.

  Some might want haute cuisine, others cheap and cheerful; some might want healthy, others just want to go to their old favourite; for others, atmosphere is important and they look for an exclusive or a vibrant or a family friendly place.

  When we communicate, we think we are being clear, but our words can hide very different interpretations: so if you want to understand the other person fully, you need to dig deeper to find out exactly what they mean.

- You listen for their values: values are the things we live our lives by, they are the things we stand for, they are the things we are prepared to make a stand for. They are things we consider good or bad, right or wrong, important or unimportant. As such, they are benchmarks against which we make our decisions.

So link your message to their values and they will be much more likely to buy into it. They will see it in the light of something that they consider good, right or important.

- And you listen for their personality type: we saw in the last chapter the power of various profiling tools that can help understand how the other person thinks. Well, you don't need computer software to do the analysis, you can just listen to how they speak. That's just what the software does anyway.

If you listen out for these, you will learn exactly how to persuade the other person. If you know their drivers, their emotions, their values, their criteria and their personality type, you can then frame your message in terms of these and now they are more likely to say 'yes'.

3.4 Listen with your eyes

People tell you how to influence them but, of course, they don't say it explicitly.

They won't give you a written list of their drivers or their values, not even a verbal one. Sometimes they are downright misleading: someone buying a car may say that 'value for money' is their main criterion but underneath they really prefer a sports car because it will impress their friends.

So if they don't tell you, how do you find out?

You have to listen deeply, behind the words, between the words, to the things that are not said. You have to listen to the repetition, the emphasis, the pause.

Listen to the non-verbals

Human language has evolved over a few hundred thousand years but we have evolved non-verbal communication over hundreds of *millions* of years. We have very deep wiring for communicating in these channels, but unfortunately the verbal channel drowns out all the others.

We need to tune back in to them so we can understand the other person more fully: the non-verbals are as important as the verbals.

You could ask me if I like Donald Trump and I could say 'Yeah!' with a snort, a wry smile and a roll of the eyes or I could say the same word with an energy, looking up beaming ear to ear. One sarcastic, the other affirmative. Verbal content identical, meanings totally opposite. All of my communication is in the non-verbal channels.

So we have to listen to the facial expression, the tonality, the gesture, the scratch of the ear, the movement on the seat, the looking away and so many other things.

We leak our thoughts all the time

Imagine the most repulsive food you can. Maggots? Cow dung? Tomatoes? (It's tomatoes for me.) If you now imagine eating that food, without doubt you will show something on your face. Even if it's only a micro-movement, there will be some kind of scrunching up of the mouth or backing away movement of the head or tightening of the throat as you feel the disgust at the thought.

We leak our thoughts all the time and if we know this, we can work it.

So you are selling a house and their face lights up when you point out the railway station is within walking distance. You can now guess they are a commuter and reduced travel time is important. Tell them they are opening a new line with a fast connection and you have your sale.

11 THINGS THAT CAN TELL US ABOUT THEM

1. The clothes they wear.
2. Their accessories.
3. The books they read.
4. The tv programmes they watch.
5. The websites where they get their news.
6. Their holiday.
7. The car they drive (or don't drive, they ride a bicycle).
8. Their house.
9. Their job.
10. The friends they keep.
11. Their partner.

All of these, and more, leak information, their values, their style, that you can use.

You need to look as much as listen. Train yourself to pay attention to these leaks and you will learn a lot.

Poker players know this.

TOP TIP

If you suspect they hold a particular value but you aren't 100 per cent certain, you can always check by saying something that alludes to it. Then gauge their response, verbal or non-verbal, and it will give you greater confidence in your suspicion.

It's like a poker player showing their cards

Michael Reddington, Certified Forensic Interviewer, Developer of the Disciplined Listening Method, President of InQuasive, Inc. Michael is an expert at moving people from resistance to commitment. He has spent over a decade training investigators on the successful application of non-confrontational interview and interrogation techniques and is the author of the book, Disciplined Listening.

'Handshakes provide a great opportunity to assess your counterpart's communication. When I meet someone and we shake hands I take note of how they behave: the distance they keep, if they step towards me, if they look me in the eye, the words they use and of course the strength of their grip. While these observations may not be definitive, they often provide indications as to my counterpart's confidence level, personality and aggressiveness.

Then, once I know their mindset and approach, I adapt mine in any number of ways to take advantage of it.

My most memorable interrogation example occurred when I had to interrogate a Director of Consumer Marketing for a national retail organisation. He was in the process of being promoted to Vice President when rumours surfaced that he was committing fraud and embezzling money. There was no hard evidence and the promotion process was already in motion. I was told quite clearly that if he confessed, he would be terminated. If he didn't, he would be promoted to Vice President.

Just another day at the office.

My client warned me the suspect was six feet, four inches tall and weighed over 250 pounds. They said he had recently lost a ton of weight and had become appreciably more arrogant. They prepared me for the fact that he liked to use his size to try and bully and intimidate people.

It's always nice when people come as advertised. When he entered the interrogation room and shook my hand, he stood so close to me the toes of our shoes touched. He gave me the death grip handshake, rolled his hand on top of mine and pulled me towards him. I literally had to look straight up to see his face. His introduction was about as dominant as it could have been.

Fine: advantage me. He very clearly tried to intimidate me before our conversation even started. I now knew that he was overcompensating for a lack of confidence and wanted to draw me into a competition for dominance. In fact, his attempt at establishing dominance actually put me in the superior position.

I had no evidence, and I knew it. If I met him head-to-head on the metaphorical battle field, I would force him to take a position that he could defend forever. My move was to take the opposite approach. Stay calm, cool and collected and let the conversation come to me.

Often the most unsettling man is the man who can't be unsettled. Once he realised he couldn't draw me into an argument, he had to listen to what I had to say. Thankfully he began confessing about 30 minutes into the meeting and wrote a multi-page written confession at the conclusion of our conversation.

When people declare their attitudes and intentions like this, regardless of what they are, they give you the strategic advantage. Like a poker player showing their competitors their cards. Once you know what they are holding, you know how to play them. Stay calm. Stay within yourself and stay focused on your goals.'

3.5 Listen with your body

Listening is a physical process. We saw earlier that people have a deep need to feel listened to and so it is not enough to listen, you need to *show* you are listening, and we saw that asking questions and using minimal encouragers will help with this. But the physical side helps too and actively looking at them, nodding our head and with attentive body language, all demonstrate you are listening and will go a long way in addressing their need to feel listened to. Now they will feel safer, they will be more likely to open up and they will be more willing to listen to you in return.

And there is more we can do physically. We have seen that reflecting back their words is part of showing you have understood them, well so is reflecting back their body language. Their body language is not random, it is part of their communication and reflecting back shows you've got it.

It is, as the word implies, a language – a surface structure expression communicating what is going on in the deeper parts of that person's brain. A couple of years ago, my young nephew excitedly described the breakfast buffet at his hotel on holiday and did a sweeping gesture with his hand as he did so. That gesture wasn't random, it expressed how the buffet was represented in his brain as a great spread of delicious food laid out in front of him. If I did something similar when I talked about the buffet, I would be showing him subconsciously that I fully understood.

So it is part of the expression of their meaning but it is more still, it is also an expression of their energy level or their mood even. We can often tell someone's mood before they say anything, simply from their body language – 'Uh-oh, they look angry' – so if we reflect their body language back to them, we are also reflecting back their mood. We are saying (at a subconscious level), 'I understand how you feel'. More than that we are saying 'I feel the same' and, even more still, we are saying 'I'm like you'. And if your intention is to help them feel significant, competent and liked, doing this goes a long way in creating this safe space for them.

Plus, taking on their body language will help you understand them better because the link between physiology and emotion is two-way. If you have an emotion, typically that leads to a specific body language which is why we can make such comments as 'they look angry'. But conversely, if you do a physiology, you will pick up that emotion. So, do their physiology – sit the way they sit or stand the way they stand – and you will pick up some of that mood.

By listening at a body language level, you are listening much deeper. It's a powerful way to listen to all those things that are felt but not actually said.

3.6 Listen with your HEART

People make decisions based on emotions, so listen out for these. Not only will it help you frame your message but it will also enable you to connect and empathise with them and identify any unsaid issues and motivations. You want to show you understand their experience and their emotions and that these are legitimate.

HEAR them

Forensic psychologists Laurence and Emily Alison have spent years studying the methods that work in such extreme contexts as interrogating suspect terrorists and repeat sex offenders. Their work is based on the approach called Motivational Interviewing, sometimes known as Behavioural Change Counselling.

They find the most effective approach to the interview is a structure they call 'HEAR',[5] which stands for:

- Honesty
- Empathy
- Autonomy
- Reflection.

Honesty means your communication must come from a place of truth and authenticity. If the other person suspects even the smallest amount of deceit or manipulation, you have lost them. Be open, even with the difficult truths; any hiding, again, means they will not completely trust you and so they will not open up themselves.

Empathy is where you show to them you understand how they are feeling. One example they give is when your toddler wants to wear their favourite dinosaur t-shirt and you say they can't because it's in the wash. This just won't cut it with the toddler, even if they put it in the washing machine themselves, and you will get a whole load of screaming in reply.

If, instead, you reply along the lines of 'I know, you love that t-shirt, don't you? That dinosaur is really scary, it's a brilliant t-shirt. Let's have a look, oh no, it's in the wash right now. It's ok, I'll tell you what we'll do, we'll dry it today specially so you can wear it tomorrow. That will be exciting, won't it? And today you can wear this other t-shirt you love' (hopefully also with a dinosaur on!). You will probably get a much happier toddler and a more successful morning.

Emotional labelling, putting words to the feelings, is very powerful. It actually reduces activity in the amygdala, exactly the outcome we are after.[6]

TOP TIP

Verbalise any negative feelings you suspect they have about you. 'You're probably angry with me because. . . I would be angry myself if that happened to me.' This gets it out in the open and it can now be properly addressed.

Then autonomy: the other person needs to have a choice and to have control over that choice. If we try to pressure them into it, they will dig their heels in further. Giving them the choice and asking their opinions about the matter show you are respecting them.

SONAR reflection

And if you thought HEAR was a great acronym for listening, how about SONAR for reflection? More helpful guidelines from Laurence and Emily Alison:

- Simple reflection: Verbatim reflection of part of what was said (and the part you choose to reflect should be the part you want them to elaborate on).

- 'On the one hand' reflection: Summarising two conflicting views the other person has ('It seems that on the one hand you're angry with them but on the other hand they're a good friend').
- No arguing: Instead explore ('Can you tell me more about. . . ?', 'I'm not quite sure I understand. . . ').
- Affirmations: Look for things you can agree with and build on ('Without doubt, Thatcher had good intentions and wanted the best for the country').
- Reframing: Reflecting back deeper feelings or values that you think might be there ('I'm getting. . . is important to you').

Listen with your HEART

I love HEAR and SONAR as acronyms; even better I love them as models. But I'm going to add one letter and turn HEAR into HEART because we need to hear with the heart. We need to bring compassion; we need to help them in their need for psychological safety.

And the T stands for Together.

We need to listen together. We need to listen to each other. We need to work hand-in-hand to solve the issue we are facing together. If it's us working together to solve the challenge we are facing, they will work alongside us to solve it.

So you need to listen to understand how they see that situation and why they behave the way they do and the reasons, perhaps quite deep reasons, behind any resistance. And once you do that and acknowledge their perspective, you can now start to work together to find the solution that works for everyone.

To say it again: if you want to change their mind, you need them to listen to you properly and process what you are saying and they will only do this if you listen to them properly and process what they are saying first.

You need to listen together and that means you going first.

You do all of this already?

'Yeah', you say, 'I'm honest. I'm empathetic. I let them decide for themselves. I never argue. I do all these things but I still can't get through to them.'

And I'm sure you do all these things but sometimes, if you aren't getting the outcomes you want, you have to do them a little bit more.

Maybe you think you're not arguing but they think you are. Maybe you think you're being honest, but perhaps you're holding back a tiny piece of information and they've picked up on it. After all, everyone proclaims honesty but they're happy to insist they can't pay more than a thousand pounds for the car when they know full well they have fifteen hundred cash in their back pocket.

Listening with your heart can be difficult, but it really can be the thing that makes all the difference.

Imagine you work in a call-centre and you have an irate customer on the phone, ranting at you because of some bad experience they had with your company. You can take it personally and get angry yourself or you can get defensive on behalf of your company, but it is only likely to cause the customer to rant more. If, instead, you wait until they finish and then apologise on behalf of your company and say how you understand their feelings and you were furious yourself when something similar happened to you recently. If you do all this, now the customer will calm down and be ready to have a proper discussion.

Likewise, if you're the person who is phoning the call-centre, you will get a much better result if you apologise for venting your feelings on them, say how you appreciate it is not their fault and you recognise it must be very difficult for them being shouted at all day.

How far should you go with it? The answer is a pragmatic one. If you've got your outcome, you did it perfectly right. If you haven't got your outcome, you need to do it more.

I was once involved in migrating a core department of a major oil company to a shared services centre and I had a meeting with the head of a particular team about migrating their roles across. The meeting went very well – or so I thought until I got back to my desk to find she had sent an email to all staff about how outraged she was by my suggestions. So I went and had another meeting with her to clear the air and this time sorted it out – again, until back at my desk I received a similar email, again to all staff.

Now this particular person was quite a high-profile, politically important individual within the organisation and these emails were not good for my reputation, let alone the success of the project. But I tried one more time. And this time, I listened to her, I really listened. I thought I had listened before but I hadn't properly. I had listened only as a pretence; I hadn't taken on board what she was saying at all. Why would I? I knew the answers already.

But of course my answers weren't going to work. So in this third meeting, I listened properly: listened out for the concerns behind what she was saying, and then changed my answers to show that I had taken them on board and I was going to protect them as well as she would have done herself.

When I got back to my desk this time, there was no email. A few weeks later, though, there was one, again to all staff. But by now she had become a champion for the project and her message told everyone what a great job we were doing and how everyone should get behind it to make it work.

HEAR and SONAR are cute acronyms, but they hold the secret to changing the other person's mind, even in extreme circumstances.

But you do have to do it, even when it's really difficult.

I do deserve better, don't I?

Richard Bryant-Jefferies, counsellor and author. Richard has spent many years counselling and supervising counselling in various settings, specialising in addiction counselling. He has written over 20 books on the topic and numerous chapters in other professional books.

In his writing he has developed a novelistic approach using fictitious scenarios and dialogue informed by his own experience as a counsellor to convey what happens in therapy. In the following piece he uses this technique.

'I remember sitting and looking at the referral letter from the GP: "street drinking. . . , chaotic lifestyle. . . , childhood history of violence in the home. . . ". Gary was in his late 30s and was struggling. I knew it was going to be a challenge.

Gary attended his first appointment. He was wary, didn't say much, clearly on edge. He had little self-esteem and, as it became clear over the many therapy sessions that followed, behind the outward bravado, his ability to feel good about himself was minimal.

He had been starved of three key developmental experiences in his early life: people being honest with him – he had experienced little of this and now found it hard to trust; people trying to understand him – no-one had listened to him when he needed them; and people showing kindness towards him – no-one had cared when he needed help.

As time passed Gary found it easier to talk. Yes, there were missed appointments, but he kept coming back, sharing the difficulties he had faced in his life. He talked, I listened. Not being cared for, not feeling safe, being angry, all came to the fore again and again.

One session stands out:

Gary had been talking about how he always seemed to end up in abusive relationships and how it made him feel.

"I can't find anyone who will really care, and I get angry."

I responded quietly, wanting to empathise but not disturb the stream of thought and feeling he was experiencing. "Can't find anyone who will really care and you get angry."

He took a deep breath and sighed. "I guess I just don't deserve anyone."

He was looking down as he spoke. I responded to what he had said, "Don't deserve anyone." I spoke with the same emphasis.

The room suddenly became very quiet. I could feel goosebumps. Something was happening, something deep. I'd had these sensations before. I could feel my eyes moistening. Hold the silence, I said to myself.

Gary looked engrossed in something. Thoughts, feelings, I didn't know what. But my job now was clear, not to get in the way.

I heard him take another deep breath that came out again as a sigh. More silence.

Gary looked up. He spoke, almost in a whisper.

"I do deserve better, don't I?"

My heart went out to him, his pain, his desperation, so many feelings etched into the expression on his face. Where do you begin empathising with that in words? I simply nodded, slowly. It didn't feel right to say anything and draw him out of what was happening within him.

A faint smile. He nodded too. Another deep breath. No sigh this time.

Things moved on for Gary over the coming weeks. His drinking was more under control. He developed greater capacity for positive self-regard and made changes in his life. Much later when reflecting on what had helped him, he recalled that session.

➤

> "That was the moment when something clicked, shifted, I don't know how to say it, but I do know what made it happen."
>
> I asked him if he wanted to tell me.
>
> "I saw it in your expression, there were tears in your eyes. No-one had ever done that, ever. And I mean ever. You understood, you cared, really cared. It made me feel I deserved something better, I *knew* that now, and I was going to get out there and find it.'"

3.7 Listen to the things that can't be said

Daniel Shapiro, the founder of the Harvard International Negotiation Program, also talks about the importance of listening for emotions in his masterful book, *Negotiating the Nonnegotiable.*[7] He points out we need to find a rational solution, but we can only do this if we have addressed any underlying emotional considerations first.

Greed, anger, ego, hate, resentment, jealousy, disgust, panic, grief will all impede finding a rational solution.

But it gets harder when the emotion is mired in a taboo, something that one or both sides are uncomfortable discussing: perhaps two siblings who get along except when the topic of their parents' divorce comes up; perhaps two friends who get on except whenever the Israel–Palestine situation is mentioned.

These can be the most difficult situations to work with and, paradoxically, also where we most want to change their mind.

Shapiro encourages us to establish a safe zone to discuss it by clarifying and communicating the intention ('Look, neither of us want to fall out here. . . ') and ask permission to talk about the taboo topic, naming it, and exploring it without any commitment from either side.

If it's too difficult confronting head on, he recommends chiselling away at it and weakening the power of the taboo.

11 WAYS TO BROACH A TABOO TOPIC INDIRECTLY

1. Talk around it.
2. Talk about it indirectly.
3. Talk about it off-record.

4. Talk about it in a less formal environment.
5. Allow a mediator to facilitate it.
6. Use humour.
7. Remind yourselves of the bigger picture.
8. Talk of the longer-term historical relationship.
9. Talk of past successes.
10. Talk of future plans.
11. Get sponsors on either side to help.

3.8 Listening and asking questions

Listening is difficult; it goes against our wiring. But there is a simple trick that helps: the question.

Our natural tendency is to dive in with our opinions. Asking a question holds us back from that and we have to listen to their answer before we dive in.

Listening doesn't have to mean staying silent, with an occasional 'I see' thrown in. We can bring curiosity; curiosity to understand:

- why they think the way they think
- why they say the things they say
- why they behave the way they behave
- why they feel the way they feel.

If you have earnt the right, the speaker will appreciate interaction and will open up. If they really get you are listening to understand and giving them the space to express what they want to express and perhaps even *helping* them express what might be a difficult thing to say, your part in the conversation does not have to be completely passive, you can ask questions and make suggestions too.

Ask, give space, listen, silence, listen, silence, ask again, is a good pattern.

Q: How do you hijack their brain?

A: Ask them a question.

The brain is wired such that when you ask a question, they can't think of anything else as they try to answer it. It is a response called Instinctive Elaboration and it is an automatic reflex, beyond their control. For that moment, they can *only* think of your question. In fact, even to decide they aren't going to answer it, they have to answer it internally.

This is powerful when it comes to influencing.

Salesperson: What do you think of this top?

Customer: Oh, it is quite nice, now you mention it.

Salesperson: Do you think it would look good on you?

Customer: *{Imagines it looking good on them}* Yes, I think it might, I'll try it on.

A study of 40,000 participants found that simply asking if they were likely to buy a car in the following 6 months increased their chances of purchase by 35 per cent.[8] Another study asking the participant's intention to vote in an upcoming election produced a 25 per cent increase in voter turnout.[9]

Asking questions about a behaviour primes the neurons for that behaviour and so the behaviour is more likely to take place.

Salesperson: Great, so you're going to take it?

Customer: *{Still imagining it looking good on them}* Yes, actually, I think I will!

In fact, asking questions about their opinion on something releases serotonin and dopamine in their brain – nice chemicals to have washing around. No wonder Karen Huang and Michael Yeomans of Harvard found that, quite simply, people who ask questions are more liked by their conversation partner.[10]

Moreover, if your questioning process means the other person comes to the conclusion themselves, they will be willing to defend that decision a lot more because they made it themselves. Autonomy.

What is a good question to ask?

Clearly, open questions will generally be more fruitful:

- 'What was your reasoning for. . . ?'

- 'What are your thoughts on. . . ?'
- 'Can you tell me more about. . . ?'

These are all great open questions which will allow the other person to answer in the way they would like to answer.

Probing questions, using the word 'specifically', are useful for avoiding misinterpretation:

- 'A small piece of land? How small specifically?'

And closed questions will remove any vagueness, the answer is yes or no, no room for wriggling:

- 'Just to be clear, did you actually get that in writing?'

You may read in some places that 'Why?' is not a good question because it triggers a defensive response. It can do but doesn't have to. As with everything, a lot of it is in how you ask it. Ask in an accusatory tone and, sure, people will get defensive.

But ask with a tone of curiosity and if you have already built a positive, supportive relationship and it is clear that you are coming at it from a collaborative, problem-solving perspective, with their outcomes in mind, they will be fine. As with everything, so much is in the intent and as expressed through the non-verbals.

So what question should we ask? Well, *that* is a very open question in itself and as such quite often a great question to ask. We can ask it of ourselves or we can even ask them.

From another angle, we might ask ourselves, 'Where do we want their mind to go?' and then think of the question that takes their mind there.

> *Where do we want their mind to go?* More focused on saving money

Question: What will happen when you hit your overdraft limit?

Where do we want their mind to go? Motivated to finish their homework

Question: What will you do after you've finished your homework?

Finding the right question isn't easy, especially in sensitive situations. If you formulate the question slowly, pausing after each word, it allows the brain to race ahead and mentally try different versions and the likely responses, so you can shape the question even as it comes out of your mouth.

But ultimately we learn by trying and by sometimes getting it wrong and then adapting.

Back to Motivational Interviewing

We have seen Motivational Interviewing (MI) already; it is a field used extensively in challenging situations like addiction and repeat offenders. It's a growing field and it's a growing field because it gets very good results even in such tough situations.

And like hostage negotiation, working in equally tough situations, its approach is based on unconditional positive regard, listening and asking questions.

MI practitioners spend a lot of time exploring the discrepancy between the behaviour and their thoughts about the behaviour. Most addicts and repeat criminals will have at least some thought about stopping, but a suggestion that they give it up will likely be met with a response of 'Love to but ain't gonna happen'.

So the practitioner will explore this and, in doing so, increase the motivation to change. They will ask:

- Questions about the drawbacks of the current behaviour

'If you don't change, how is this going to impact your life?'

'Well, I'm going to spend most of my life in jail.'

- Questions about the benefits of change

  'But if you were able to change, what would that help you do?'

  'I could live a normal life, I could see my kids, I could play football for my local team, I could go on holiday, just like everyone else can.'

- Questions about their motivation

  'What is the main reason for you to change?'

  'It's my kids. I've hardly seen them grow up. I've let them down. I hate that.'

- Questions about how they will go about the change

  'So what do you think you could do this time that would be different to previous times?'

  'I suppose I could sign up for the support programme. I've never really bothered with that in the past, I didn't think it worked. But I guess it's down to me to make it work.'

- Questions about next actions

  'That's great. So what do you think you'll do to put this into action?'

  'I'll sign up for the programme. I'll do it this afternoon. I've got the paperwork already but haven't done anything about it. I'll do it this afternoon.'

They have to choose the solution. Without this, their change of mind won't last – the offender will sign up for the programme but not attend; your neighbour will turn their music down this time but it will be just as loud next Friday; your child will do their homework today but tomorrow there will be even more resistance.

Now this raises the stakes – not only are we getting them to change their mind, but we're getting them to do it out of choice – but it is the only outcome that will last.

3.9 Listening and the Vulcan Mind-Meld

So what goes on in the brain when you are listening? Lots! Who knew?

We've already seen how important the amygdala is in the process and something else that takes place when someone listens to a speaker is neural entrainment, sometimes called interpersonal synchrony.

This is the process by which two brains become synchronised and fire in the same way. For example, when two people's movements are aligned, their motor neurons will fire similarly and this can be seen in functional magnetic resonance imaging (fMRI) scans of the two people's brains. Likewise, when they sit or stand in the same way.

It turns out this synchrony increases trust, co-operation, helpfulness, empathy and other pro-social behaviours, and the kind of behaviours you would like to see when trying to change someone's mind.[11]

But it is not just motor neurons. Any movement is likely to be related to other brain areas too – a facial expression might be expressing an emotional response, which itself might be linked to a specific belief. So, through entrainment, the other person's neural gestalt is also likely to come into synch too, i.e., their emotion and their belief.

It goes further. Professor Uri Hasson at Princeton found that when people's speech is correlated, so too are the parts of the brain governing speech and, indeed, many of the higher parts of the brain involved in what's being said as well.[12] Other studies have shown that emotions amplify this effect.[13]

Hasson also found that the more the brains were synchronised, the more successful the conversation was considered, as judged by those taking part in the conversation.

So you really do want to synch your brain with theirs.

Miles Davis said 'If you understood everything I said, you'd be me' and there's a truth in this. The closer your brain is configured in the same way as the other person, the closer you are getting to being them. Is this the basis of the Vulcan Mind-Meld? Who knows?

And in persuasion, the more your brains are synchronised, the more you can then lead that dance of synchrony and bring them with you where you want them to go.

In summary

We need to listen more and better. Shift your attention to them – you've already persuaded yourself; you need to focus on them if you want to know how to persuade them.

- Whatever behaviour you want them to do, you have to go first

  If you want them to listen to you and engage with your ideas, it makes sense that you need to listen to them and engage with their ideas first.

- Come from a position of love. Or at least respect

  Their resistance to engage with your ideas largely comes from a lack of psychological safety. They have to feel psychologically safe with you. Always show respect, no matter who you are talking to. Even the ones you think don't deserve it. And love is even better.

- Listen to understand, not refute

  Stop listening for the 'Yeah, but. . .' opportunity – that doesn't work; it only gets 'Yeah, but. . .' back. Instead, listen to really understand them.

- Listen deeply

  Listen out for their drivers: what they want; what they don't want. Listen out for other emotions. Listen for their values and their criteria. All of these will help you get your message across more successfully later on.

- Listen for the non-verbals

  Much of their communication is in the non-verbal channels so tune into these and you will learn a lot.

- Address any emotions

  They will only hear your great logic if you address the emotion first.

- Ask more questions

  Questions are great – they elicit useful information; they engage the other person and they help influence. What's more, they help us listen.

- Synchronise your brains

  At a deep subconscious neural level, the more your brain is in synch with theirs, the more they will think you are 'one of us', the more psychologically safe they will feel in your presence, the more likely they will listen to you and agree with you.

Gary Noesner, one of the creators of the modern hostage negotiation approach, says listening is the cheapest concession we can make.

It helps give them the feeling of psychological safety which is critical for them being open to change their mind.

But to do this well, you have to feel psychologically safe yourself. So let's look at that.

Be strong

4.1 Build your strength so you don't have to use it

Let's be clear here: many persuasion contexts don't need strength and often it is downright counter-productive.

If you've read this far, you'll know the whole premise of the book is that it is generally something you want to avoid. If you're a boss and demand your team member stay late ('Why?' 'Because I'm your boss and I say so'), it might work once, but that relationship is going to go south rapidly. You've just lost a lot of relationship capital.

Let's be clear, too, that we aren't saying build your strength to use it.

In the world of negotiation, there is a big myth that it is all about power. But if you try to push something through just because you can – the other side may agree because they have to but they will quietly find a way to even things up. They will put their juniors on the job; they will use cheaper materials; they will cut corners; they will follow the letter of the agreement rather than the spirit; they will put horse-meat in the burger instead of beef. Win–lose rapidly becomes lose–lose.

Nor are we saying bully the other person into your political views or threaten them into changing their mind: it simply doesn't work.

So why be strong?

Strength, though, has its place. It gives you the psychological safety you might need to take the approach outlined in the previous chapter, which isn't always easy in a disagreement. To give them psychological safety, you need it yourself.

Operation Journeyman, below, is a brilliant example of this. This secret naval deployment enabled the British negotiators to be very clear in their communication that the government was willing to defend the Falkland Islanders' interests and enabled them to be very confident in holding that position. As a result, a military confrontation (in 1977, at least) was avoided.

Being strong helps avoid a fight. As I said in the introduction, it's amazing how collaborative the other person will be if you have a bigger army than them. If they are now being collaborative that, in turn, enables you to be less defensive and more generous.

So here is the nub: we are not saying use your strength; we are saying build your strength precisely *so you don't have to use it.*

The Falklands War averted

Lord David Owen, Foreign Secretary 1977–1979 and MP for Plymouth for 26 years. He also held posts as Navy Minister and Health Minister and was co-founder of the Social Democratic Party and its Leader from 1983–87 and 1988–90. From 1992–95, he served as EU peace negotiator in the former Yugoslavia and co-authored the Vance–Owen Peace Plan.

Below, he describes Operation Journeyman.

'The possibility of an Argentine invasion of the Falklands was getting ever more imminent, and it reached a critical point we could no longer ignore. We spent long meetings in the Defence and Overseas Policy Committee of the Cabinet discussing our options and, at the end of November, a secret naval deployment was dispatched to the area. Not long after they arrived, the tension lowered and by Christmas they were on their way home again. Hostilities had been averted.

This was 1977. There had long been a recognition at government level that perhaps the status of the islands did need to change but it was very difficult to find a solution that was politically viable, and the Falklanders and, indeed, the general British public were firmly set against it.

The activities of the Argentine junta, who had seized power in a military coup a year earlier and were responsible for thousands of deaths and disappearances in that short time, didn't help their own cause. The Islanders had no wish to swap a relatively stable and peaceful democracy, even if 8000 miles away, for a dictatorship that tortured and killed its opposition.

As a consequence, talks between the two countries over the status of the islands were moving very slowly and the Argentines seemed to be losing patience. Events were escalating: the British Embassy in Buenos Aires had been bombed; the Argentinian Navy had shot at an unarmed British research ship, the *RRS Shackleton*; and they had set up a "scientific" post on Southern Thule, British islands under dispute and the so-called "scientists" all wore military uniforms.

This increasing belligerence was also evident when they arrested several Soviet and Bulgarian trawlers in the area and Argentinian relations with Chile were deteriorating. The net result was a real risk of the talks due in December in Buenos Aires breaking down in acrimony and the Argentine Navy setting sail to invade the Falklands. While they could reach it in a matter of days, the Royal Navy could not get there in under three weeks.

A meeting was held chaired by the Prime Minister following my request that a Royal Navy hunter killer submarine should be sent secretly to lay in wait off the Falklands in case of any invasion. The Ministry of Defence felt it essential to be able to communicate with the submarine and to do this they wanted two frigates and two support vessels. But in discussion it became clear they did not need to be close to the Falkland Islands but could be mid Southern Atlantic outside the range of any Argentinian reconnaissance planes. Great trouble was taken to keep the deployment of all the ships secret and the reason was a simple one. We envisaged that we might have to do this more than once if tension in the negotiations reoccurred.

Clear rules of engagement were established with the assistance of the Law Officers. If Argentine vessels ignored repeated warnings and advanced close to the Islands then the submarine commander was authorized, as a last resort, to fire a torpedo at the oncoming vessel.

Now, with this insurance policy in place, our negotiators could confidently take a more robust line at the negotiation table. In the event, the next round of talks actually went reasonably well and the vessels were withdrawn and their deployment never leaked. A year later a repeat exercise was considered but was not felt necessary.

Had the submarine and ships not been there, it would have been harder to be so convincing that the British were prepared, despite not having an airfield, to defend the Falkland Islands. It was a great shame that in early 1982 a repeat of such a naval deployment was not even seriously considered. Parliament only heard about the 1977 deployment during the first House of Commons debate when the Argentinians had already landed on the Islands.'

4.2 And strength can mean many things

When we're talking strength, we're not saying force or the threat of physical violence.

Professor Ivan Arreguín-Toft,[1] a Fellow at Harvard, is a military historian. He studied 200 wars where one army was at least ten times stronger than the other. Not surprisingly, he found that in most cases the larger power won.

However, he delved deeper. He saw that in many examples, the weaker party recognised the imbalance and chose an unconventional strategy in response. In these situations, the weaker party won nearly two-thirds of the time, despite the massive power stacked against them.

So the lesson is to be creative in terms of your power source.

9 THINGS WE MIGHT MEAN WHEN WE TALK ABOUT STRENGTH

1. Doing your research and knowing the details of the situation inside out.
2. Having the confidence to put your case across clearly in a situation you might otherwise be nervous.
3. Coming up with the idea that makes the breakthrough.
4. Staying robust when the other person vehemently pushes back.
5. Staying calm when others are losing their temper.
6. Staying resilient in the face of a major setback.
7. Listening when you would really rather strangle.
8. Recognising you might be wrong sometimes.
9. Taking the higher road, staying resolute in the ethical approach. Virtue, itself, is a strength.

It can mean so many things. I worked with one lawyer with a client involved in a family will dispute. There were seven claimants and his client was ready for a battle in court but this would have been costly and she had a very weak legal case so was unlikely to win.

However, the facts of the matter did suggest she had a strong moral position. So they drew on this power source instead. She appealed to the other side's benevolence and wrote a very personal letter from the heart, without any legal references, and in this way she was able to persuade all six other claimants to agree to her claim.

Power is more a creative process than a violent one.

How much personal strength do you have?

Much of it is personal. As a trainer in the field, I spend a lot of my time telling 'nice' people to toughen up (and an equal amount of time, by the way, telling others to soften up). The niceys needn't worry about being *too* tough: their own conscience would never let that happen.

Too many people ask for their pay-rise but the boss growls without even looking up so they run quickly back to the safety of their own desk and that's that for another year.

Stand up for yourself! What's the worst that could happen?

- Project strength. Not aggression, but a quiet confidence that communicates there is no point in trying anything on.
- Project credibility, whatever credibility might mean in your world. I knew one person who built a business as an interior designer to the world's elite. She learnt how to fly a helicopter because it signalled she was at home in that world. 'Meet you on your yacht? Does your yacht have a helipad? Great, I'll see you there.'

- Project the right status. You don't want to be over-bearing but you do want to project enough.

  Human beings are pack animals and status is important, so important that we evaluate it in approximately 40 milliseconds (about one tenth of the time needed for the fastest conscious decision).

  The attributes of status will depend on your culture (what's considered high status in a law firm might be different to a football team) so you might want to consider if there's anything you need to boost your perceived status, however you might do that in your particular context.

- Know your stuff. The more you have done your preparation and know the situation inside out, the less likely they will try anything on.

TOP TIP

Get feedback. Feedback can tell us those things that we don't know about ourselves and if you don't come across as strong as you could, feedback will let you know and will tell you how you can improve.

Get James Bond on your side

Chris Bryant, MP for Rhondda. Chris served as Deputy Leader of the House of Commons and Under-Secretary of State for Europe and Asia. He was also Shadow Secretary for Culture and Shadow Leader of the House of Commons.

'I remember when Burberry decided to close its factory in the Rhondda, the management made lots of mistakes, including suggesting they were going to close the factory on Christmas Eve and giving every member of staff £20 as a Christmas present which could only be spent in a Burberry shop (all that could buy you was a scrunchie).

The GMB Union, Leighton Andrews (the local Assembly Member) and I ran a strong campaign with national newspaper stories every week. At one point Judi Dench announced she wouldn't accept a BAFTA that year if it were sponsored by Burberry so BAFTA had to find a new sponsor.

Of course we knew we couldn't stop the company if they were determined, but we wanted to get a much better redundancy settlement for the workers, some extra months' employment and a big donation for local charities in the Rhondda.

At the first meeting between the company and the campaign, I let slip that I knew Daniel Craig, the actor who plays James Bond. When the GMB and I turned up for the final meeting, the chairman conceded the first two of our demands fairly quickly, but seemed more reluctant about the cash for local charities until I mentioned Daniel again.

He clearly feared that 007 would come out against Burberry and agreed to give us £1.5 million and double the redundancy terms, as long as I could guarantee that Daniel wouldn't say a word.

Since I hadn't even mentioned it to Daniel, I was happy to give Burberry the guarantee they sought.'

4.3 Be strong on the outcome, soft on the approach

Hostage negotiators work in extreme circumstances: often a life-or-death situation, emotions running 11 out of 10 and polar-opposite demands.

And yet they get very good results. How?

The first thing to point out is they never actually negotiate. They never say, 'Kill all ten hostages? Let's split it 50–50, you can kill five and release the rest'.

The second surprising thing is the softness of their approach. Most crisis negotiators use a standard model called the Behavioural Change Stairway, a simple five-step model developed in the 1990s by Gary Noesner, later Chief of the FBI Crisis Negotiation Unit.[2]

It does exactly what it says on the tin: it is a stairway, a step-by-step process, to behavioural change. The five steps are:

1. Listen
2. Show empathy
3. Build rapport
4. Persuade
5. Behavioural change.

That's pretty soft. Whenever I run a workshop with hostage negotiation in the title, everyone gets really excited: 'Great, I'm going to be like Denzel and Bruce, cool!' And then I talk about listening and showing empathy and they are surprised. Hostage negotiators get their great results by being very strong on the outcome but being surprisingly soft on the approach.

The model, in fact, is almost identical to the Motivational Interviewing we've seen in counselling. Both models are based fundamentally on deep listening, unconditional positive regard and building as much psychological safety as possible, so that the other party can own the solution themselves. And both models get great results in extreme circumstances.

Now, of course, hostage negotiators have a SWAT team in place and that helps. But it is exactly this that allows the negotiator to use a more sympathetic method. Similarly, it's your strength that enables you to take the soft approach which is most likely to bring about a sustainable result you are after. Speak softly and carry a big stick, said Roosevelt, and it is the big stick that allows you to speak softly.

What if I don't have a SWAT team?

But you might well be thinking, 'What if I don't have a SWAT team?'

Well, we saw in the previous section that strength and power are creative processes, so maybe you do have a SWAT team but you just haven't recognised it yet. Maybe you can find a SWAT team from somewhere.

Maybe it's even your lack of power which is your source of power; this was something Nelson Mandela used to his advantage. In the last weeks of his imprisonment, the South African government wanted to release him but he refused to leave until he had been granted all his requests because he knew his very imprisonment provided much of his negotiation leverage.

But what if you've racked your brain as much as you can and you really don't have any obvious power? It's possible.

Then double-down on everything else. We've devoted a few paragraphs to the SWAT team, there are 200 other pages in this book focused on the rest. If you have enough strength, you don't have to use it; but equally, if you use all the other tools outlined in the book well enough, you won't need the strength either.

And maybe these *are* your sources of power. Maybe it's your ability to listen, your ability to build rapport, your ability to provide psychological safety in a world where the other person has rarely felt it which is your strength.

We spent a lot of pages in the last chapter talking about Motivational Interviewing and there was never any talk of strength or SWAT teams.

The last source of power

But maybe even the Motivational Interviewer does have a SWAT team. Maybe the status quo is their SWAT team – the addiction, the return to jail, the threat of a wasted life.

So as long as you are willing to walk away, you too have a source of power. If you aren't, and they are, you have zero power and you have to accept any terms they demand.

> **TOP TIP**
>
> Always be willing to walk away but don't do so lightly. Stay focused on your Why Five Times outcome and walk away if the alternative will help you achieve it better.

- If your boss is categorically saying no pay-rise this year, perhaps it is time to look around for better paid jobs elsewhere.
- If your dispute with your neighbour is getting nowhere, perhaps a signalled willingness to consult a lawyer can make them more amenable to an agreed solution.
- If the vendor of your dream house simply isn't budging on their asking price and it's a figure you really can't afford, perhaps you go back to the market and look for another dream house.

Just the very fact you are considering the alternative might be what makes the other person take you seriously and start negotiating. And if not, fine, go ahead and walk away – again, to emphasise, if and only if it really is going to help you achieve your 'Why?' outcome better than what is currently on the table.

And in a political conversation? Being robust on your outcome doesn't mean sticking to your opinion and desperately insisting they change theirs, stopping only once they've agreed you're right in everything you say about everything. You can agree to disagree and this will keep the relationship open for further discussion later.

And being robust on your outcome doesn't mean you can't change your own mind either. In a political conversation, your outcome should be the truth, not vindication of your opinion.

Have a strong 'no'

Now being strong on your outcome means being able to say 'no'.

If you are very clear on what you want, as discussed in Chapter 1, it makes it easier to distinguish between what you can say 'yes' to and what you need to say 'no' to.

But you still have to be able to actually voice it.

I worked with one client who told me she 'needed to get her life back'. When I pressed for more details, she said she had stayed at work until 3am twice that week and until 10pm the other nights: 3am wasn't normal, she said, but 10pm was.

It turned out her problem was her inability to say 'no'. She was in-house legal counsel for an investment bank and was very good at her job and very conscientious. People would ask her to do tasks that really weren't within her role but because she couldn't say 'no' she would take them on. And because she was conscientious, she would stay until 3am to get them finished.

She had to learn to say 'no'. Her homework was to practise in front of the mirror, pointing her finger and saying sternly, 'No, no, no!'. She said 'no' to this and I was pleased she was making progress.

Now, contrast her example with that of an ex-colleague of mine who ran the internal IT Helpdesk for a large insurance firm. The phone would ring, he'd pick it up, growl a little, then say 'no' and put the phone down. I asked him if he was the Helpdesk, where specifically was the help in that conversation and he said people had to learn to do their own job themselves.

He told me when he first joined the company, everyone called the Helpdesk about everything and obviously the previous incumbent had said 'yes' to everything. 'Fluff on your screen? Oh, I'm sorry, I'll come down and wipe it off.' My colleague knew he had to re-train people to call him only when it really was a problem for him to deal with. And to be fair to him, everyone knew his bark was worse than his bite and when it did come under his remit, he would growl a bit more but then he would fix it.

But by having a strong 'no', he was one of the most productive people I'd ever met. He single-handedly did the support and development for a massive computer system and when he left, he was replaced by a team of twelve.

Being strong on the outcome and soft on the approach does require the ability to say 'no' – although maybe in a more diplomatic way than growling.

Killing with kindness

Koen Schoenmakers is the Co-Founder and Chair of the Positive Impact Society Erasmus University.

'It was the start of Covid, when no-one was allowed to go out, so everyone felt locked up. We had a small balcony and we could climb from there on to a roof which caught the sun. Of course, we weren't officially allowed to: the council had decided it was breaking their regulations so they put a ban on it, but in the circumstances it was a lifesaver.

One day I was chilling on the roof and I coughed, for no particular reason, and my neighbour, who was in his garden, heard this and made some passive-aggressive remark about staying inside and not spreading germs.

Later that evening my room-mate sat on the balcony with her boyfriend and the neighbour started shouting at her, telling her to remove all our stuff from the roof. It ended up in a complete screaming match. My other room-mate was furious and flipped straight into war-mode, planning all kinds of things to do, like playing loud music through the night, for no reason other than to annoy the neighbour.

I was worried, though: he might call the municipality, which would mean the end of our roof. So I tried something else.

The next day, I bought a plant and attached a note: "Hey, let's talk, here's my phone number", that kind of thing. I rang his doorbell, expecting a fight from him but I was ready to "kill him with kindness" as my tactical response. He answered and when he saw the plant, he started to tear up! He was completely taken by surprise by the gift because he too had been expecting a fight.

When I saw this, I realised we were simply two humans trying to make the most of our difficult situations. We ended up having a long chat and found we had a lot in common: we both played music and we both had similar views on many topics. He was a single father of three girls, one of whom had Down's syndrome, and his business had been impacted a lot by the lockdown so he was very stressed and scared about the situation for his daughters.

Later, he sent me a long text which I can summarise as "Super sorry for my behaviour, I was wrong and you were right". He had lived next-door for 18 months and we'd never really spoken to each other before. Now, thanks to the plant, we talked and both went well out of our way to be good neighbours.'

4.4 Dealing with difficult people

Being strong on the outcome also requires you to be able to deal with difficult people, otherwise you might burst into tears at their slightest snarl and you've just lost your outcome.

I'm sure you don't have any difficult people in your world but in that hypothetical instance that you did, what should you do?

It's worth understanding where the difficult behaviour comes from and people often employ such behaviours tactically because they have found it's worked for them in the past. If you show it won't work on you, there is no point in them continuing it.

As an example, I once had a very tall, physically imposing delegate on my course. When he was asked what he wanted from the course, he said he would like some negotiation skills. He said, 'I think I'm quite a good negotiator already. If anyone ever disagrees with me, I lean forward and then they agree with me!'.

'But', he continued, 'that doesn't always work and then I don't know what to do.'

And here is the lesson: if someone is rude or aggressive or manipulative or anything like this, it is usually because they have found it works for them. If you don't let it work on you, they'll have to do something different.

11 WAYS TO DEAL WITH DIFFICULT BEHAVIOUR

Bismarck advised, with a gentleman, be a gentleman and a half; with a pirate, a pirate and a half. And this is not dissimilar to our twin-track approach of SWAT team combined with softly spoken hostage negotiator. But it doesn't need to be quite so binary, we can be more nuanced than this. We might

1. Ignore it
2. Smother them with kindness
3. Call them on it offline
4. Call them on it publicly
5. Distract them or change the subject
6. Take a time out
7. Hand over to a partner
8. Warn we will walk away from the deal
9. Use humour
10. Get angry ourselves
11. Show how upset we are.

Do anything else we can think of that could get us our outcome.

Stay in control of our behaviour and do anything we can think of that could get us our outcome. Behavioural flexibility is crucial because we can never predict with certainty the best approach; but the greater the range of behaviours we have available to us, the more likely we will succeed.

Managing your reaction

Of course, this isn't always easy. When they do that thing that presses our deepest buttons, it is easier to get offended, outraged, upset, scared, any kind of deeply wired emotional reaction. But we need to make sure we don't go down that route because if we do, we are no longer in control of our behaviours.

We can use emotions but make sure we are in control of them. As John Lydon said, 'Anger is an energy'; but equally, as

Aristotle said, 'Anybody can become angry – that is easy; but to be angry with the right person, and to the right degree, and at the right time, and for the right purpose, and in the right way – that is not within everybody's power and is not easy'.

Two great philosophers we can learn a lot from.

So how do we stay in control of our reaction? Let's be clear. Yes, it's hard, but it is something we can learn to do. Sometimes we can even see it happening in slow motion and one part of us is telling ourselves not to respond in the way we always do but another part goes ahead and responds anyway. Don't get frustrated here: this is the learning process in operation, and you have just moved one step closer to mastering it.

Awareness is key. Awareness that it happens and, specifically, *how* it happens with you. We all have our own triggers and our own unhelpful responses, and the better we understand them, the slowed-down split-second-by-split-second process of them, the more effectively we can intervene to prevent it happening.

TOP TIP

Go to the balcony. What is going to the balcony? It is to imagine you are in a cinema and you take a seat in the balcony and you watch your situation on the cinema screen. From this 'fly-on-the-wall' perspective, you can give yourself advice on how best to proceed.

TOP TIP

Plan a response beforehand. If we expect a trigger situation ahead of time, we can put things in place to avoid it or respond differently when the situation occurs.

We can label our reaction (our funk, our ego, our chimp, our inner child, our defensiveness), and it then becomes a solvable entity and we can even bring it up with the other person which will enable both of us to work together around it.

And always, always, always we need to stay in touch with our main outcome and ask ourself which behaviour is most likely to help achieve it.

It helps when we remember that their behaviour is not personal. It might *seem* as if it's personal but it is actually driven by the situation and their desire to get their outcome. You are simply the person in the way of them getting that outcome (as they see it) and this is why it seems to be aimed at you. It is just a tactic that they have found has worked for them before.

Time, the great healer

Time also helps, so managing your reaction when you're communicating via email is easier. Don't respond instantly: let your mood calm down before you hit send.

Personally, I've noticed I go through multiple stages of de-escalation of my mood. I might be furious at first and my initial draft will probably include swear-words but my second draft removes them, replacing them with sarcasm. The third might be ice-cold logic but then my last draft will bring a bit of warmth back in and it is only this version that has any chance of persuading.

3 WAYS TO MANAGE YOUR REACTION

If we do have time before we respond, we have other strategies available to us to help shift the mood.

1. Imagine your friend in this situation, what would you advise them to do?

2. Write down a list of pros and cons of staying with the mood and a similar list for achieving your Why Five Times goal.
3. Ring a friend and talk it through with them.

Rather than sit and seethe or wallow in our indignation, these will be more helpful for getting our goal.

Learning from lobsters

Perhaps the best way, though, is to pre-empt the behaviour and this way you don't actually have difficult people in your world. And if we do everything we've discussed to date – we aim high for both parties at the 'Why?' level, we know our stuff inside and out, we are showing unconditional positive regard, we are listening deeply to their points, and at the same time we have our own personal strength and robustness – we are reducing the likelihood of any difficult behaviour.

In this respect, we can actually learn a lot from lobsters; in fact we can learn a lot from their sex lives. Lobsters, we know, have a very hard and knobbly shell to protect them and there is a problem with this: it stops them having sex. It's a bit like humans trying to have sex while wearing a deep-sea diving suit. It's not easy. Apparently.

So to get around this, the female sheds her shell when she is ready to reproduce. However, this has its own complications – now she is no longer protected and we all know unprotected sex is dangerous. For female lobsters, unprotected sex can mean being eaten by her lover. Doesn't usually happen with humans; does with lobsters.

So how does the safe-sex-minded lobster get around this? Well, she uses chemical weapons: she sprays a pheromone into the male lobster's cave which makes him less aggressive.

She can now get out of her shell and do the do, safe in the knowledge he won't attack her before she grows another shell.

That chemical is the lobster version of oxytocin.

Professor Paul Zak[3] is one of the founders of the field of neuro-economics and one of the first people to recognise the importance of oxytocin in the process of trust. Sometimes known as 'the bonding chemical', it is perhaps best known as the factor that makes the mother bond with her new-born baby. It's also the chemical that goes through the roof when two people meet and fall in love. And tails off over a five-to-seven-year period. Which explains a lot in my life.

Oxytocin, it turns out, is the biological substrate for trust.

Zak's experiments showed a direct correlation between levels of oxytocin and levels of both trust and generosity. It is contextual, of course, and nuanced – neurochemicals are highly complicated. But in economics games based around trust, Zak showed generosity increased by 80 per cent under the influence of oxytocin.

So what causes its levels to go up or down and is there anything we can do to increase it in the other person so we can trust them more?

Firstly, some things have a negative impact. Zak conducted an experiment at a wedding where he baselined everyone's oxytocin levels beforehand and then again on the day and he found everyone's oxytocin went up in direct proportion to how close they were to the bride. That is, the bride's went up the most, the bride's mother the next and so on. With one exception.

The groom!

Now, to be fair to the groom their oxytocin levels did increase, just not as much as we would expect from our model. And the reason was that their testosterone also increased, after all they were the man for the day, and testosterone is an oxytocin inhibitor. So anything which boosts testosterone will impair trust – competitive behaviour, macho behaviour, too many men around!

But if you want to increase levels of oxytocin in someone else, it turns out that one of the simplest ways is to act trustingly towards them.

One economics game Zak studied was the Trust Game. In this, Person A is given $10 and is told they can give some of that to Person B. Anything they give will get tripled in value and Person B can then decide to keep it all or give some back. Person A has to trust Person B's generosity.

When Person B was shown trust, they returned 50 per cent more than when simply given money randomly by a computer. What's more it was a linear correlation. The more money given (i.e., the more they were trusted), the higher the oxytocin surge in the recipient.

13 THINGS THAT CAN INCREASE OXYTOCIN

Increase their oxytocin and their trustability by:

1. Showing trust in them
2. Appropriate touch (e.g., a light touch on the elbow)
3. Rapport-full chat
4. A moving story
5. Friendly games
6. Joining in gossip together
7. Dance
8. Having friendly people around

9. Having pets around
10. Finding something in common with them
11. Giving them chocolate, red wine, fatty foods or other comfort foods
12. Placing emphasis on the collaboration and shared goals
13. Using 'we' and 'us' language.

All of these have shown in different studies to raise oxytocin levels. They may not all be possible in your deal but the more of this kind of thing, the better.

Harvard Business School Professor Leslie John, in her work on detecting lies, also found that pro-social behaviour on our part leads to better behaviour on theirs.[4] For example, she found people are less likely to lie to those they like and trust and if someone shares sensitive information (i.e., shows trust), the other person is less likely to lie here too.

Increase oxytocin, increase trust, decrease difficult behaviour.

4.5 Physician, heal thyself

But before we start labelling everyone as problematic, maybe the problem is with ourself. I have a friend who is very sensitive to people who eat loudly and everywhere she goes she finds them; I'll be in the same place and I just won't notice.

If you are particularly sensitive to difficult people, you will find them.

We often go into the conversation expecting an argument and then, surprise, surprise, we get one. Perhaps if we expected a good conversation, *that's* what we'd get instead.

In my early 20s I had a relationship that was quite fiery. We would spend most evenings arguing: I would say something, she would say something cutting back, I would say something equally cutting and so on. I'm sure you know the script.

Then one Friday I went around to her apartment, bracing myself for another combustible night. In my mind I ran through all the arguments we were going to have and I was angry even before I arrived.

But I noticed this is what I was doing and I decided to behave differently this time. I decided she couldn't touch me, that I was going to be in a good mood all the time no matter what she said. I was going to ignore any barbed remark and if (and, as I expected, when) it got too much, I would just walk out and that would be that. I wouldn't even say anything as I left, I would simply smile and take my coat. End of.

I knocked on the door. She answered it with a big smile, really pleased to see me. We both said some really nice things about how the other person looked, we both laughed a lot about different things and we had a lovely evening. No argument. I learnt a powerful lesson.

Their behaviour is partly a function of what you bring to the relationship – if you bring difficult behaviour yourself (I know, unlikely), you will get more of it. But if you bring a positivity to it, that too is what you will get.

TOP TIP

If you find yourself angry with them even before the meeting, it's probably in your head and not in the real world. Instead, visualise the meeting going really well with them responding positively and everyone happy with the outcome. It will be much more likely to go well if you do this.

So if our boss hates us and gives us more work than the laws of physics allow, if our colleague blocks everything we do or even think of doing, if our finance director slashes our budget out of spite, while smiling and increasing everyone else's at the same time, instead of coming out all guns blazing or hiding in the toilet, perhaps it is wise to consider a different strategy and bring a more positive energy to it ourselves.

Steven Spielberg recounts the story of how he was bullied when he was 13 years old by an older kid at school. His response was not to run away or fight back. Instead, he invited the bully to play a role as a war hero in a film he was making. They became friends.

We need to be psychologically safe too

This isn't easy and, as we've seen, our brain gets hijacked by unhelpful emotions and we revert to fight or flight, a strategy developed several hundred million years ago and, to be honest, needs updating.

But if your behaviour comes from fight or flight, they are unlikely to feel psychologically safe and so are unlikely to be in a place where they are open to changing their mind.

And what's important here? Is it showing them how angry you are? Is it getting revenge? Of course not, it's about getting your outcome and the emotional hijack is almost certainly going to sabotage this.

So you must make sure you feel psychologically safe too so you can bring that positive energy. Look after your own well-being and your own self-esteem.

Here, again, we are saying our strength is important – not to use against the other person but to use *for* them (and, indeed, therefore for us too). Our strength provides us with a sense of security that will engender magnanimity rather than a fear-based aggression.

And in moving from fear to magnanimity, from blame to support, we are also moving from effect to cause. While blame often feels very pleasurable, it diminishes our power.

With blame, we are on the effect side of the equation: we still have a problem on our hands and it is dependent on the other person's limited capability (from the perspective of our blame) to resolve it. If we drop the blame, it allows us to move to the cause side of the equation: we can now take responsibility for getting the outcome we want.

Dropping blame increases our power in the world.

TOP TIP

Give yourself what it is you need to feel secure and strong so that you, in turn, can provide strength for them, so they feel safe.

Should I apologise?

Magnanimity is not weakness, it is strength. Similarly, apologising can seem a weakness but in actual fact it can come from strength.

In the commercial world it is often considered a dangerous practice because it indicates admission of responsibility and therefore likely to lead to a legal claim against you. But it is more complicated than that. A 2004 study[5] by Fiona Lee and colleagues at the University of Michigan found that companies who apologised after a mistake performed better in the stock market than those that didn't. Another study by Ben Ho and Elaine Liu found that doctors were sued less if they apologised.[6]

The apologies need to be full, however. In one experiment, identical scenarios and settlements were presented with either no apology, a partial apology (expressing sympathy but not admitting responsibility) or a full apology admitting full responsibility.

When no apology was issued, 52 per cent accepted the offer but when a partial apology was offered, the number accepting went down to 35 per cent. However, 73 per cent accepted the full apology. Uber found similar results when they conducted a big data experiment on apologies.[7] Led by their chief economist, Professor John List, they sent out various types of apology emails to a dataset of 1.6 million passengers who arrived late. The partial apology, not taking any responsibility, made no difference when compared to the control. However, a full apology with a $5 coupon to make up actually led to more Uber use than before the error.

I once worked with some lawyers with high-net-worth clients. They were involved in a divorce case where one side was demanding $100m, the other side was offering zero. My guess was an apology would have been worth $50m straight off.

If it gets you the outcome you want, why not? Sometimes you have to get over yourself first before you can win them over.

The strength of humility

Which all points to one thing: humility, intellectual humility. After all, we could be wrong. I used to believe in Santa Claus, you probably did too; I suspect you don't anymore. Even as an adult, I've changed my views on many things. I may have to change my opinion on this current belief that I am right now shouting from my soapbox and banging the table over.

As Oscar-winning screenwriter William Goldman said about Hollywood, 'Nobody knows anything'.

Now you might be thinking your three PhDs qualify you to disregard humility but, interestingly, the 'I'm not biased' bias tends to be more common among intelligent people than others. Plus, there is always Dunning–Kruger.

The Dunning–Kruger effect is a treasure among cognitive biases and says people with low ability tend to overestimate their competency at a task. In meaner terms, stupid people are too stupid to know they are stupid.

But before we start laughing and pointing fingers at others, the first rule of Dunning–Kruger Club is that no one knows they are in Dunning–Kruger Club. The second rule is that everyone is in it.

Ray Dalio, founder of the world's largest hedge fund, Bridgewater Associates, identifies two key obstacles that prevent us achieving better results and he describes them in his excellent book, *Principles: Life and Work.*[8]

The first is the blind spot which we all have because we can never study a topic enough to know it completely. Despite all our experience and certainty, none of us can know. The second is the ego which, again, we all have, driven by very deep processes in our brain that want us to feel safe.

His answer to both is the same: radical open-mindedness. Always be conscious you might be wrong, that despite the certifications and diplomas coming out of your ears, other people can show you things you did not know, whatever their pay-grade. Replace your need to be right with the joy of learning what's actually true, knowing this process of learning is never ending.

TOP TIP

Be open to the fact you could be wrong. Ask what evidence would show that and look for this evidence. You will do better with this approach than by assuming you are right.

Humility doesn't mean soft, it doesn't mean unambitious, it doesn't mean shy. It simply means being aware that what we think is true may not be after all. This is empowering, it enables you to find real solutions which you wouldn't look for otherwise.

Philip Tetlock found in his research on superforecasters[9] that success in predicting future outcomes was less a function of intelligence or subject-matter knowledge and more a function of your willingness to accept you are wrong and update your beliefs.

The biggest and brightest of us. . .

. . . is really not that big or bright.

A typical person involved in a conflict is less than seven feet tall and they live on a planet which is 25,000 miles around its circumference, receiving all its energy from the sun which is 93 million miles away. That is an awful lot of arguers laid head-to-toe.

And there are 200 billion similar stars in our galaxy and there are 125 billion galaxies in the known universe. As Powell and Pressburger put it, 'This is the universe. Big, isn't it?'.

Oh, and some physicists suspect there are an infinite number of universes. And that is really big.

So be humble. The world is bigger than you. An overly-sensitive ego comes from weakness; it is strength which enables humility and humility, in turn, is a strength.

Ending A Civil War

Juan Fernando Cristo, Colombian lawyer and politician and ex-President of the Senate of Colombia. He was Interior Minister from 2014 to 2016 during the time of the peace negotiations with FARC and played a major role in those negotiations.

I interviewed Señor Cristo who told me that he was in Athens, as Colombian Ambassador to Greece, when he heard the terrible news that his father had been assassinated by Colombian rebel forces. Of course, it was unbelievably painful, they had only just celebrated his daughter's third birthday together and now he knew he would never see him again. He flew back from Athens to Frankfurt and from Frankfurt to Bogotá and on the plane he had a long time to think about it, his mind full of all kinds of thoughts, and he had to decide how to respond. He told me he wanted to hate but wasn't sure this was the best way.

17 years later he found himself, as Colombian Interior Minister, negotiating with the FARC guerrillas and, of course, he had to face it all again. Civil war negotiations are the

hardest of them all and the talks were going slowly but President Santos upped the pressure by setting a deadline. They worked around the clock trying to reach an agreement, different people sitting around different tables discussing different parts of the negotiation. There were formal talks, there were talks at dinner, there were talks in the corridor.

And he began to get to know them a bit better. They talked about FARC politics, about their families, about their life-stories. He said it was tremendously eye opening to see these people, who he'd only seen in the media as criminals and responsible for terrible acts, to see their humanity.

It became clear they wanted some dignity in the agreement, to have some peace in the final years of their life and to share their last years with their families, their wives, their children. But they were very afraid, they thought signing the agreement would be signing their death warrant: 'We are going to sign but we are sure they will kill us.'

So a very specific chapter was put in the agreement to address exactly this. They set up a 'Security and Protection Corps' under the National Protection Unit, which was dedicated to guarding them and keeping them safe. And it was ultimately this that enabled the peace.

In 2017, after 55 years of war, FARC disarmed themselves and handed over all their weapons to the UN, it was an incredibly historic moment.

Señor Cristo told me that on that plane back from Athens he decided not to look for revenge, not to live with his heart full of hate, and instead to work towards reconciliation and peace in the country. And his family – his mother, his brothers – all decided the same, not to live the rest of their lives in hate but on the contrary to use the experience as fuel to work towards peace.

➤

'My country's wellbeing,' he told me, 'my country's peace, my country's future were more important than our need for revenge.'

Interestingly, he said that it wasn't easy but he knew it was the right decision, not just for his country, but for his family, for himself. His daughter was three years old, shortly after he had a boy. He didn't want them to live in the same country as he lived. They needed to grow up in a different country, a different Colombia, one that knew peace. To look for revenge wouldn't help his children, it wouldn't help him. It was a very practical decision.

'This was 24 years ago. Every year since, I write a letter to my father and I publish it in the newspaper. And every year I tell myself this was the right decision.'

In summary

Strength can be helpful when it comes to changing minds because it provides you with the psychological safety you need to be magnanimous to them.

- Build your strength

  Not to use it but precisely so you don't have to use it. The stronger you are, the more collaborative the other side is likely to be.

- Strength can mean many things

  Be creative with your sources of strength and remember it is about personal strength as much as anything.

- Be strong on the outcome, soft on the approach

  Always stay focused on your goal and be flexible in achieving it. It may mean you have to have a confident no and it may mean you have to be willing to walk away from the deal. If the latter, don't walk away too quickly – evaluate if the alternative is better than the current deal in terms of your 'Why?' outcome.

- Dealing with difficult people

  Don't take their behaviour personally. Difficult behaviour is just information; revisit your outcome and consider, in the light of the behaviour, what is your best way of achieving it and have a range of options available to you.

  Pre-empting difficult behaviour is better than dealing with it so build the relationship and trust and the problem won't arise.

- Their behaviour is often a function of our behaviour

  Consider how we are contributing to any contrary behaviour of theirs and try to bring a more positive input. It will likely bring a more positive change on their side too.

- Deal with the emotional hijack

  Our brain easily gets emotionally hijacked and while there can be a pleasure in our indignation, it doesn't get us our goal. Instead, always stay focused on what we're trying to achieve and that will help us manage our response most effectively.

- There is strength in humility

  We don't know everything; humility is our best way to understand a world much bigger than us. This may mean generosity; this may mean an apology. Both come from strength and both are strengths in their own right.

And from this position of strength, you can now be confident in working together with the other person to find a solution that suits everyone.

5 Co-create the solution

5.1 The solution doesn't exist with any one person

If you want the other person to own the solution, they must have a share in it.

Tell them to mow the lawn now and they may just point-blank refuse. But get them involved in finding a solution and they might tell you they have other commitments right now but they are free to do it later on. Great, you have your outcome.

This works at home and it works in business too. For example, in recent years marketing has moved in the direction of co-creation because the greater involvement of the consumer in the development of the brand builds much greater brand loyalty as well as being able to leverage better customer insight.

And in a parallel context, the NHS specifically encourage patient involvement in decisions about their health and care because evidence shows they will then:

- report greater satisfaction with the services they receive
- experience less regret about the decisions they have been supported to make and are more likely to say that the decisions made were most appropriate for them

- make fewer complaints than those who were not involved in decisions.[1]

So, get the other person involved in coming up with the solution.

Reframe it as a collaborative, problem-solving process

In negotiation, to get a sustainable outcome, we have to change our approach from the old-school arm-wrestle, where the strongest person wins, and reframe it as a collaborative problem-solving process, where the problem is:

- you have an outcome in mind; they have an outcome in mind
- you have real constraints; they have real constraints
- you have resources you can bring to the table; they have resources they can bring to the table.

Put all of these out in the open and then work together to solve that equation so that all parties get their outcomes, given the constraints but given the resources too. In other words, work together to create a solution that meets everyone's needs and then you can trust that the solution will be implemented.

> **TOP TIP**
>
> Make it sound as though it's their idea, now they'll fight for it.

A political discussion is just the same: it's still about identifying the real problem to be solved, the desired outcomes, the constraints and the resources and then deciding on the best solution.

Again, you won't get the best solution until those parts of the equation are accurately identified. Most such conversations make little progress because everyone is arguing at cross-purposes. Much better to find something you can agree on and work back from there.

Politically opposed Friend 1:	At least we can agree that we both want to make the world a better place.
Politically opposed Friend 2:	Yes. And the best way to do that is to boost the economy.
Politically opposed Friend 1:	Sure, as long as we do it in a fair and sustainable manner.
Politically opposed Friend 2:	Fair enough. Which means. . .

Of course, it might shift *your* position – but wouldn't that be great? It means you've just learned something new.

Going first again

Now, as we have already seen, this relies on you going first in all the kinds of behaviours you want them to do like listening properly and being open to change their mind.

It is the same with sharing information. There is a prevailing myth, in negotiation at least, that you should not share information because they will use it against you. In reality, however, the more information is shared, the better the solution reached.

Of course, you, being a highly intelligent and knowledgeable reader, will know the value of sharing but your counterparty might be more married to the myth. So, again, you need to show them the example. You can't blame them for being deceptive or holding back information if you are doing the same.

Collaboration is an investment

And if we do work in this collaborative problem-solving manner, not only do we resolve the situation at hand but we also set up a better working relationship for the future.

In 1978, President Sadat of Egypt and Prime Minister Begin of Israel signed the historic Camp David Accords and, in doing so, found a way of working together. A year later they signed a peace treaty that brought an end to 31 years of war. The Sinai was de-militarised, diplomatic relations were established, boycotts lifted and trade resumed. Two deadly enemies became allies: an alliance that has lasted to this day.

Maybe your deadly enemy could become your ally?

Leave their identity alone!

Nothing will close down collaboration quicker than threatening their sense of identity. And yet trying to change their mind can do exactly that.

William Zartman, the great negotiations academic, Professor Emeritus at Johns Hopkins University and Chairman of the International Peace and Security Institute, says we should never try to negotiate a belief system: we should negotiate *within* the belief system.[2]

Trying to change their belief system, their world view, their identity or their style will take forever, if not longer; save your energy and work with what they give you.

If you are a Democrat talking to a Republican or vice versa, or you are an anti-vaxxer talking to a vaxxer, you aren't just changing their opinion; their opinion is based on their life situation, their friends and family around them, their life history, their very sense of self. Good luck with changing that!

And if they feel their sense of self is endangered, they will go into tribal mode, into 'us vs them'. It has now become personal and it's very bad news if you're trying to change their mind.

So their sense of self shouldn't be threatened.

3 WAYS TO PROTECT THEIR SENSE OF SELF

1. Connect the new belief to their identity.
2. Connect the new belief to a different part of their identity (e.g., football fan not Manchester United fan).
3. Focus on the similarities between you.

My sister told me a story of how she got her work colleagues to finish a long Monday morning whinge-fest by joining in and then saying, 'Wow, we're being really negative here, aren't we? Let's be a bit more positive'.

If she'd told them to stop being negative, as I'm sure she was tempted, it would have put an 'us vs them' barrier up and would have got nowhere.

And in the historic Oslo Accords, one way that the Israeli and Palestinian negotiators were able to build a connection was by joining together in joking about their Norwegian hosts. Clearly you need to be careful with this and it's important to point out that the Norwegians themselves encouraged it, but it enabled them to reduce the differences in their identity and increase the commonalities.

'I don't like that man; I must get to know him better'

As this quote from Abraham Lincoln expresses, our resistance to collaboration or plain dislike often comes from not knowing the other person. Get to know them and 'actually, they're not so bad after all'.

This is never more evident than in silo-based organisations. Any comment of 'Oh, the *x* team are useless' (where *x* = IT, sales, finance, legal, support, HR, compliance, back office, front office, Head Office, Paris office or any team that isn't the team of the person making the comment) is symptomatic of such an organisation.

Nearly always these issues disappear instantly if the teams have a chance to actually meet and talk to each other. Whether that involves a social event or flying the Indian team over to meet the Head Office or simply putting photos and bios on the intranet, it will all help towards breaking down the barriers and improving the collaboration.

Build the alliance on-site

If you want to persuade, nothing beats you and the other person having direct experience together of the situation you want changing. This way you build the alliance in the face of the real-world challenge.

In the book, *Influencer: The New Science of Leading Change*,[3] the authors describe how Mike Wildfong, a manager at an engineering firm, wanted his team to implement work safety measures more stringently.

So he took them on a volunteer day to help out an ex-colleague who had been injured on the job and was now surviving on disability cheques.

They spent the day fixing things around the home for him and it was a successful initiative all-round: helpful for the ex-colleague, a bonding day for the team but, perhaps most importantly, attitudes to workplace safety transformed from then on.

5.2 Planning the process

There is no magic wand when it comes to changing someone's mind, but if you want to maximise your chances of success, you would do well to plan the process and, best, plan it together.

In complex peace negotiations this is essential. Before the talks start, there will be talks about the talks and in especially sensitive situations there are even secret talks about the talks about the talks. This leaves as little to chance as possible. One commentator on the Colombian peace negotiations said, 'We can see the light at the end of the tunnel. The problem is we don't have a tunnel'. It's the talks about the talks about the talks that can build that tunnel.

It could be you need a pre-meeting meeting with the person whose mind you want to change, to discuss how things might progress. Alternatively, it could be you just do this with your own team to make sure everyone is on board. A friend of mine who worked for a large engineering firm told me of a meeting he attended with a prospective business partner in which a very junior team member confided, 'We're so glad you're talking to us – no one else is interested and we're quite desperate'. Admirably honest, perhaps, but probably didn't help their cause. This is the kind of trouble that can be avoided with a pre-meeting meeting.

You may also want to pre-seed ideas so they don't come as a surprise. People rarely change their opinion on first exposure to an idea but, if given the chance to ponder it beforehand, they are more likely to agree; more likely, even, to claim it as their own – a result you should cheer.

I once coached two people who were jointly applying for a chief executive role, as a job-share, at a well-known public organisation. They had some great ideas about how to bring this traditional organisation into the 21st century but when I asked how the chairman, the key decision-maker, would view these ideas, they frowned. Apparently, he had an extremely conservative outlook on such things. So the majority of the coaching was spent determining how they could get these ideas to him before any interview so he would already be well persuaded of their value. They were able to identify several people they knew: people who would be willing to champion their ideas, who had upcoming meetings with the chairman and seeding the ideas through them became the basis of their strategy.

Have a meta-conversation

And as with the solution, so with the process: you will get better results if you involve the other person in defining the process. This is known as a meta-conversation: where the conversation is about the conversation itself – how it will proceed, what will be covered, what you will do if there is disagreement or if it gets heated and so on.

If you agree this collaborative process with the other person upfront, everyone is much more likely to stick to it and you can refer to it as you go through it to make sure everyone stays on track.

Gary Noesner said he would always agree with the hostage-taker how the situation would end in as much detail as he could. 'The cars will be parked here. I'll give you the signal then you will release the first two hostages. . . ' always checking in, 'Is this ok with you? Is there anything you want to change?'

If he did this, talking them through the process beforehand, he would find there was actually rarely anything they wanted to change and, when it came to it, they would follow the process as agreed and it would end smoothly.

The meta-comment, breaking the fourth wall of the conversation, is a useful device *during* the process, too, if things ever do go off track.

Smooth them through the process

There is something hypnotic about talking people through a process. Airline pilots use this effect: 'We're going to be flying at 32,000 feet, we will arrive in Miami in 3 hours' time, shortly after 5 pm and the temperature will be a very pleasant 26 degrees Celsius'.

Why do this? Are they expecting someone to say, 'I'd rather fly at 31,000 feet'? Passengers have no need to know this information, but many do have a need to feel they are in safe hands. A calm pilot with a late-night radio voice talking smoothly through what is going to happen next, telling them the future no less, helps relax any nerves.

Salespeople use this to their advantage, too, before closing a deal. 'So, the next steps would be for us to come around and measure up; we can give you a more accurate quote then. You'd make your final choice on the colour scheme then we would order the stock. It will take about two weeks to arrive. Our contractors would be on site for about a week to fit it. I would suggest letting it dry off and settle in for a couple of days, then after that it is yours to drive away. How does that sound to you?'

Personally, I have no idea what this salesperson is selling but I can answer their question: 'Yes, it sounds good to me!'. Their confidence in how the future is going to unfold exudes authority and experience and I feel comfortable with it and I'd buy three.

How to persuade someone to jump from a very high crane

Many years ago, this process was so persuasive it made me do my first ever bungee jump. I am not ashamed to admit I was petrified. I was in a cage attached to a crane and, as the cage rose, the jumpmaster talked me through what was going to happen. 'Ok, so when we reach the top, I'm going to open this gate, you're going to put your right hand here, you'll put your left hand here, then you're going to shout "1-2-3 bungee!" and you'll jump.'

In my head, I thought 'Oh no I won't, I'm actually going to ask you to take me straight down again'. But a strange thing happened.

He timed his speech perfectly so it finished exactly as we reached the top and he continued his instructions without pause. 'Ok, I've opened the gate so now put your right hand here', which I did, 'and put your left hand here', which I did, 'now shout "1-2-3 bungee!" and jump', which I did! I also shouted other words straight after, words I won't repeat here, but I completely surprised myself by the fact I followed his suggestion.

It was the quickest way down, anyway.

Lead them through the process

So, as with the jumpmaster, awareness and control of the process doesn't stop with the planning: it's important all the way through.

Start by vocalising the intention of the meeting ('We're here to agree on/to talk about/to find a solution to. . . '). If that is clear and agreed, and repeated whenever the conversation gets tricky, the chances are you will get your outcome.

Then manage the conversation through each stage: 'Ok, I think we're agreed on *x*, shall we move on to *y*?', always checking it's ok with the other party. This keeps everyone in the collaborative frame of mind plus their involvement will mean they will be less likely to dispute it later on as they have an equal ownership of the solution.

Typically, the person who informally chairs the process in this way will be the most influential person in the meeting and so is more likely to get their outcome.

TOP TIP

Start the meeting by suggesting an agenda and asking if this is ok with them.

Boost your influence bank account

And doing all of this builds the credit you have in your psychological influence bank account. According to this model, you earn credit every time you:

- say something that makes sense
- show your understanding of the other person's concerns
- help them achieve their goals
- suggest something that leads to a successful outcome.

On the other hand, you lose credit every time you:

- suggest something that doesn't make sense
- focus only on your own concerns
- block or impede the other person
- suggest something that does not succeed.

As with any account, you want as much credit in there as you can get so, quite simply, make sure you do lots of things on that first list and don't do anything on the second.

Involve people in the details

Gary Noesner, FBI hostage negotiator. Gary spent 23 years as a hostage negotiator for the FBI and was Chief of their Crisis Negotiation Unit. He was technical consultant on the Netflix series, Waco, *and was one of the main characters in the series. He developed the core hostage negotiation framework, The Behavioural Change Stairway, and wrote the best-selling book,* Stalling for Time: My Life as an FBI Hostage Negotiator.

'It's my view everything is based on a relationship. Before we get to solve a problem or spout our message across, we first have to build a relationship of trust and project our genuineness or sincerity or trustworthiness.

But there's also a question of process and if you can lead the process, you can use this to your advantage.

Back in 1993, I flew to Lucasville, Ohio to help sort out a major prison riot that had been going on for several days. The riot actually involved three distinct groups - a black criminal gang, a white racist criminal gang and the third were a black Muslim gang - and they didn't get along with each other.

Each group had different hostages, held separately. Each group wanted different things: some wanted to talk to their girlfriend, some wanted just to rant and rave about prison conditions, it was all over the place. And the more people got involved in the talks, the more chaotic it had become.

So I told the prison authorities that instead of dwelling on 'You better surrender', we needed to help them get organised.

And this is what we did. We conveyed to each group that we wanted to engage with them but we couldn't do that until they created a list of things that were important for their group. They nominated a spokesperson and then we could arrange a meeting where we would listen to them properly and understand their issues.

And so we set up a meeting. I told the authorities, "Your mission in this meeting is not to tell them what you want them to do, it's to listen to what they have to say. Acknowledge their point of view. You don't have to agree but you do have to acknowledge". And they did that.

After the meeting, there was a list of 20 or so points and the authorities' gut response was to say they couldn't agree to any of them because it would set a precedent: "Nobody tells us what to do".

But when we went through each point, it was amazing how easily each could actually be put into practice. The rioters had clearly followed our direction and had put the requests in very polite terms, along the lines of "We would like you to look into getting better food for the prison canteen", "Please look at elongating the recreational time" and so on.

Now this prison facility did have a history of unusually harsh methods and this was the backdrop to the riots. In my view, these requests, as presented, were a golden opportunity. I told the authorities, "You can do each and every one of these. You don't have to implement the findings, but it's easy to look into them. And if you can't implement them, give a reason why you can't".

The prisoners agreed to release the hostages and to surrender. So we moved to the next stage and went into long conversations about the details of exactly how they would surrender, "You'll line up here, we'll take 10 people at a time. . . " and so on.

When you involve people in the details of the process, always checking in – "Is this ok with you? Is there anything you want to change?" – then you actually find that there usually isn't anything significant they want to change. And now they have agreed to it, they become partners in its implementation and success.

And that's what happened. The hostages were released and the inmates surrendered.

We managed to resolve such an inflammatory situation not through the forceful imposition of authority, but through willingness to be open and listen and through the effective management of the process. It was in showing respect and in allowing the other parties to feel a certain amount of vindication and success in the matter.'

5.3 Be creative

So it's a problem-solving process, but sometimes solving the problem isn't that easy.

This means you need to be creative and come up with as many ideas as possible, because who knows which one is going to be the right one.

Creativity was invented in 1942 by Alex Osborn, the advertising guru. Well, if not creativity, he did invent the word 'brainstorming', using it first in his book *How To Think Up*[4] and developing its principles further in the more popular *Applied Imagination: Principles and Procedures of Creative Problem Solving.*[5]

4 PRINCIPLES OF BRAINSTORMING

1. Go for quantity: it is easier to whittle down than think up.
2. Withhold criticism: suspending judgement for a later phase of critiquing enables people to free their thinking.
3. Welcome wild ideas: they just might lead to another idea that would not have been generated otherwise.
4. Combine and improve ideas: it is the generative nature of the process that will develop the optimal solution.

This is one time where a meta-conversation about these principles is especially important: 'Let's fire all the staff' is fine in a brainstorm but may get a different response if no one else is in the same space.

Identify as many variables as you can

One thing that will help the creativity a lot is to identify as many variables as possible. Let's see what exactly we mean by this.

You ask for a promotion and your boss's response is a great big 'no' because you haven't made it easy for them to say 'yes'. But the situation isn't binary, promotion or no promotion, be creative and identify more variables. Instead of just the job title:

- there is the salary, the bonus or other parts of the package that could be brought into the conversation
- it could be attending the board meetings
- it could be working on better projects
- it could be other forms of recognition for the extra work you've been doing
- it could be working 4 days a week
- it could be working 6 days a week.

A million possibilities, limited only by your imagination. And, in the spirit of the chapter, two imaginations working together is better than one.

Your client says they can't afford your quote so either you work at an unprofitable rate or you don't get the work at all. But, again, the situation isn't binary.

- You could reduce the scope to fit their budget.
- You could push back some of the work to your client, or subcontract it out or pass it down to someone more junior.
- You could give them the Dacia version of the service rather than the Rolls Royce.
- You could use cheaper material.
- They could pay upfront to help with your cashflow concern.
- They could wait until your quieter period.
- They could sign up for a greater amount of work.
- They could bring referrals.
- You could be price dependent on the outcome.

A million possibilities, limited only by your imagination(s).

You're trying to lose weight and your partner suggests you both go out for dinner. You, of course, don't want to as you think of all the calories you'll put on. So long as it's a binary choice of 'Go to restaurant' or 'Not go to restaurant', one of you will be disappointed. But there are other variables that might help.

- You could choose a restaurant with a healthy option on the menu.
- You could agree to the restaurant tonight and tomorrow your partner cooks a low-cal meal in return.
- Or you're happy to let your partner go for dinner with a friend instead.
- Or you go for a run together to burn off some calories first.
- Or your partner agrees in return to join you on a portion control diet for a while, knowing this will help you with your commitment.
- Or they agree to let you know when they'll be around to eat for the rest of the week because that will help you plan your food a lot better.

A million possibilities, limited only by your imagination(s).

In the dying days of the Soviet Union, as glasnost and perestroika opened up a failing economy to many western businesses that wanted to trade there, creativity was often the name of the game. Pepsi wanted a part of the market and agreed to sell $3 billion worth of soft drinks but there was a shortage of foreign currency to pay for it.

There was no shortage of ageing military equipment, though, so Pepsi accepted 17 Soviet submarines, a cruiser, a frigate and a destroyer as part payment instead.[6]

Maybe your client can offer you a submarine as part payment? I'm just saying maybe.

Go visual

It's generally a good process to think with ink.

The problems we have to solve are often quite complex with many components, with all kinds of cross-connections and dependencies, and it can be too much to hold in our brain for the period of time required to solve them. So, getting the problem out on paper will make this task a whole lot easier.

This is even more true when the problem lies across two or more brains. If you need to communicate a complex idea to the other person, going visual will help a lot.

You don't need to be Picasso: simple shapes and lines and stick-people will work (mind you, that reminds me of Picasso). You can represent ideas, people, relationships, entities. You can use them to explain, to explore, to put a structure to the situation, to create new ideas. You can point to them, you can link things, you can move things around.

'Un bon croquis vaut mieux qu'un long discours', said Napoleon – a good sketch is better than a long speech. And when it comes to changing minds, it's probably true.

Leverage the differences

Typically, we will value these variables differently and this is often where the solution lies.

According to Harvard professors David Lax and James Sebenius, by collaborating you find that the differences that might otherwise lead to conflict can be the very things that provide value. In their book *The Manager as Negotiator*,[7] they advise leveraging those differences and how you do this is, again, limited only by the imagination(s).

5 WAYS TO LEVERAGE THE DIFFERENCES

1. Difference in interests: Maybe one side is after a political result and doesn't care about the budget; another doesn't care about the politics but is focused only on the money. They can easily find a solution that suits everyone.
2. Different predictions of the future: I own a stock and think its price will fall; you think it will rise by 10–15 per cent. We agree you buy it now for 5 per cent more than the current price and we are both pleased with the deal.
3. Different views on risk: I'm risk-adverse so take a guaranteed outcome; you're happy with a gamble so take a performance-based figure with a higher potential upside.
4. Differences in time preferences: you can have it now if you pay full price but it will be cheaper if you can wait till the off-season.
5. Different resources: you have a cow, I have a bull, together we have a business.

It is in these different prioritisations or valuations of the variables that we can find the 1 + 1 = 3 solution upon which nearly all progress is made.

How do you pronounce 'Nene'?

Paul Chard, Chairman of Northampton Croquet Club, who found a creative way to resolve a local dispute.

'How do you pronounce the River Nene? As it happens there's a disagreement about that and we found a "creative" way of resolving the disagreement.

The river starts in Northamptonshire, flows through Peterborough and then out into the sea in Cambridgeshire. At the Northampton end, it's pronounced as in rhyming with "ten", but by Peterborough, it rhymes with "keen". There's even a town in the middle, called Thraxton, where it's pronounced differently on each side of the town and, in fact, there are people who live in the middle of Thraxton who have family arguments over it.

Both sides can produce maps and history and academics that support their argument. So how do you resolve it?

By playing croquet, of course.

You see, I'm Paul and I'm the Chairman of the Northampton Croquet Club and I have a friend, another Paul, who is Secretary of the Peterborough Croquet Club. Two clubs at either end of the river and we always have a joke about its name.

So we decided to play a challenge match between us and the losing team would have to adopt the pronunciation of the winning team for the next 12 months.

And we made it a pride issue, representing your town and the river. God and Her Majesty are on our side, for England and St George, all this kind of thing! Lots of banter, all raising the stakes.

And it got a lot of attention. We sent out a press release for the local media and they picked up on it straightaway. The Northampton newspaper called me the Good Paul and my friend Bad Paul while Cambridge Radio, of course, had it the other way round.

But we took the game seriously. Everything was formalised, we had a handicapping system, we wore our official croquet clothes: it was fun but serious. The match was really exciting, as it turned out, they were all well-balanced matches and the thing about croquet is that it can't be a draw so it was close all the way to the end.

➤

> And we won! Peterborough will now pronounce it nen, to rhyme with "ten", for the next 12 months until the re-match. Radio Northampton were very keen to hear Paul say Nen on air but Radio Cambridge didn't ask so I brought it up myself: "Sorry Paul, I didn't quite hear that, can you say it again?!"
>
> It was a bit of fun and it was a light-hearted way of resolving an issue in these times of opposing views on so many topics. And it was some good publicity for the game and for our clubs.
>
> Next up? Is it scones or scones?!'

5.4 Focus on Why Five Times

We saw in Chapter 4 that you need to be strong on the outcome and soft on the approach but that doesn't mean you should never budge an inch from your position. This is perhaps the most common myth in negotiation and the problem with it is that if both sides are 'good' negotiators (i.e., tough), nobody budges so nobody gets a deal: a deal that could benefit both parties is lost because neither side is willing to shift.

Even if the sides do begrudgingly move to meet somewhere in the middle, you might end up with a result where neither side is happy: one side thinks they sold it for a steal and the other side believes they paid way too much. Many people think splitting the difference is win–win but we can see here it's actually lose–lose.

Quite apart from this, if you're a tough negotiator, your reputation may go before you and people will either not want to work with you or – if they really have to – will factor it in accordingly. That 20 per cent discount you got – maybe, unbeknown to you, they had first hiked the price by 30 per cent.

So we (borrowing the Royal 'we' briefly) do not recommend this approach.

And, at the same time, we don't recommend rolling over either. Instead, be firm but flexible.

Firm, and this is the key point, on your Why Five Times goals, but flexible on how you achieve them.

So don't give them that discount just because they're more stubborn than you and don't give it to them because they are banging the table and you don't want to upset them. Clients are very clever and even if the product was free, they would still ask, 'Can't you do better than that?'. It is their job to try, it's just part of their script and it's your script to say 'no'.

Stay focused on Why Five Times

On the other hand, do give them the discount if, in the variables, you get something of equal or greater value in return and this enables you to reach your Why Five Times goal.

Google, Facebook and other tech companies give lots of their products away for free; that is a *big* discount. But now they own your data and that means they own your future and they are well on their way to their Why Five Times objective of global domination. It was a master-stroke, if slightly evil. (We recommend master-strokes but not evil ones, not even slightly evil ones.)

In 2020 in the Ukrainian city of Lutsk, an armed gunman carrying grenades boarded a local bus, taking the 13 passengers hostage. Police cordoned off the area and a siege developed in which shots were fired and the hostage taker, 44-year-old Maksym Kryvosh, clearly unstable, threw explosives out the window.

How was the stand-off resolved? Kryvosh promised that he would release the hostages and give himself up if the Ukrainian President, Volodymyr Zelensky, posted a video on Facebook recommending people watch the Joaquin Phoenix 2005 film *Earthlings*, a film about human cruelty to animals.

The president willingly did this and Kryvosh kept his word. Within the hour, the crisis was over and the Facebook post was removed, replaced by a note thanking the police and anyone else involved in ending it.

Zelensky gave in to the demands and was criticised by some in his country; a more conservative President might have deemed it unbecoming, but it was quite simply a pragmatic way of getting his outcome – the crisis was resolved and lives were saved.

(At the time of writing, Russia has just launched its invasion of the Ukraine and President Zelensky is making a remarkable stand against their forces. Let's hope the pragmatism and creativity he showed in Lutsk, along with the efforts of other parties, will help bring about a peaceful solution as quickly as possible. Sadly, it is looking very bleak at the moment.)

Closer to home, as we saw in Chapter 1, maybe the Why Five Times goal isn't about changing their mind at all. Is it really so imperative to change your parents' minds on how to vote? Maybe it's more important to show that you love them. Do you really have to change your friend's views on the Occupy movement? Maybe it's better to keep them as a friend.

Stay focused on Why Five Times, what's really important.

5.5 Conflict resolution

What if things have got heated and it's become an argument, even a fight?

Well, you can try to win the fight if you like, but that's another book. We're here to get you your Why Five Times goal and winning the fight is a distraction. In this book we recommend you stay focused on your Why Five Times goal and do whatever you need to do to get it.

This will probably mean managing your response – perhaps dropping the outrage and the desire to fetch your machine gun – which isn't always easy.

And it will also mean dropping the blame. There's no point in trying to fix the past; there is only any value in solving the current problem so you can get to where you want to be. And this will only happen if you move away from 'I'm right and you're wrong'.

6 WAYS TO MANAGE THE CONFLICT

1. Look for any opening in the conversation for a de-escalation.
2. Meta-comment: 'We can carry on arguing but that probably isn't going to help anyone; alternatively, we can calm down and look for a solution'.
3. Re-focus on interests: This isn't helping either of us. . .
4. Accusation audit: You're angry with me because. . .
5. Take a time-out.
6. Make a joke.

Forgive?

In some situations, we may need to forgive too. Maybe a real event has happened that cannot be undone but we have to move on from it if we want to progress.

We have deep wiring for revenge but this just leads to an endlessly destructive cycle of tit-for-tat behaviours leaving everyone worse off. To put an end to this we need to forgive, but this is not easy.

In *Negotiating the Nonnegotiable*,[8] Daniel Shapiro studied exactly these situations and made several recommendations.

4 WAYS TO HELP FORGIVING

1. Do an analysis of the pros and cons of forgiving and nearly always it will recommend forgiveness.
2. Build connections personally, at a human-to-human level, by finding out about their lives, their history, their family and their interests.
3. Share your story and be genuinely interested in theirs.
4. Work alongside each other to make progress.

Shapiro also says that, if it's easier, perhaps you don't need to forgive but just decide not to get revenge. This might lead to progress and then a time, later, when you are more ready to let it go.

But if you want them to de-escalate, guess what, you have to go first. If you've read this far in the book, you knew that sentence was coming.

Respect their sacred

Shapiro's work also looks at when the argument arose because we disrespected something they hold sacred – maybe we laugh at their reference to the Bible or we tell them they worry too much about their child's health.

To navigate these situations, he recommends taking the time to understand the other person's sacred topics: asking questions about them, proactively and demonstrably respecting them and talking *within* that belief system. And even if you don't agree with them, you should always acknowledge the reverence they hold for them.

If these are openly acknowledged and respected, there is often room for manoeuvre in them. For example, they may originally insist the other party has no access to the children at all, but after discussion and acknowledgement of any underlying fears they may now allow access in such a way that those underlying fears are addressed.

You can also find overlaps in the sacred (e.g., our two religions have the same god; we both believe honouring the traditions of our ancestors important; we both want the absolute best for our kids) or build a common sacred that both parties can honour: now it is 'us' instead of 'me vs you' and we will be able to make better progress.

Allow face

Given ego is so important, allowing face can be really important so give them a route out of it that keeps their status intact. Help them find a face-saving justification for their change of mind, so they can still feel good about themselves and can justify it to anyone else they may need to.

In fact, you may even give them a victory if it's not that important or let them appear to win.

Sir Christopher Wren built the famous Guildhall at Windsor (the venue, several centuries later, for the wedding of Prince Charles and Camilla Parker Bowles), which has a grand meeting room built above an outdoors corn market. The story is said that the council who commissioned the building were afraid it would fall down and crush the market below so they asked him to put in some more pillars for support.

He refused, perfectly confident in his ability to construct a building that would stay up for centuries. The council, however, insisted and, since they were paying for it, he reluctantly gave in and built four extra pillars.

The story continues that it was not till many years later that workmen putting up scaffolding to decorate the ceiling saw that none of the four pillars actually touched the ceiling! Wren had let his sponsors think they got their way, but in actual fact, he had kept to his original engineering, knowing that posterity would side with him.

Now the story may or may not be true but the lesson is clear: sometimes it is worthwhile letting the other party get their way, even if it is really only for show; sometimes help them look good in front of their people if, in the end, it means you get your outcome.

And and

In the conflict, there is almost certainly truth on both sides. Both of you contributed to the argument, both of your ideas have value in them, both of you have a valid perspective, both of you have been upset by the other.

The route to resolution is to find the truths on each side and you do this by exploring, asking questions to understand and listening attentively to the answers, as discussed at length in Chapter 3.

Then any solution must incorporate both truths, demonstrably so, and a great way to do this is to use the word 'and'. 'And' enables two distinct, perhaps apparently contradictory, ideas to be held at the same time without any one of them weakening the other.

In improvisation, actors are not allowed to use the word 'no' because it is too destructive, instead they say 'Yes and. . .'. Let's say you want to build a scene that involves a dog and the other actor says 'Oh look, there's a cat', you can't say 'No, it's a dog' because the scene will degenerate into an argument. Instead, say 'Oh yes, and look, there's a dog too'. Now you have an interesting scene developing.

'No' means conflict; 'Yes and. . . ' generates solutions.

In their book, *Difficult Conversations: How to Discuss What Matters Most*,[9] Harvard authors Stone, Patton and Heen talk about 'The Third Story' – that story that is not yours, not theirs, but what a neutral mediator may tell after hearing both sides. Telling this third story can be what allows both of you to move on from the conflict and find agreement.

The word 'and' will be central to this story.

To borrow their great example, let's say you are delivering the news you are breaking up with your partner: 'I'm breaking up with you because it's the right thing for me *[give reasons here], and* I understand how hurt you are and that you think we should try again, *and* I'm not changing my mind *and* I understand how you think I should have been more clear about my confusion earlier, *and* I don't think that makes me a bad person, *and* I know I have done things that have hurt you, *and* I know you've done things that have hurt me, *and* I know I might regret this decision, *and* I'm still making it *and. . . and. . . and. . .* '.

Of course, you wouldn't deliver such news in this lecture kind of way, but the example illustrates nicely how situations can be complex, with many perspectives, each legitimate, perhaps contradictory and the word 'and' allows each their validity.

It is our ability to operate in complex, contradictory spaces that enables us to resolve or, better, avoid conflict.

Don't break up with us!

Jo Hemmings, Behavioural Psychologist and expert Relationship Coach. Jo has been voted Dating Coach of the Year multiple times and has also sat on the panel. She is consultant psychologist on a number of television programmes and Assessment and Duty of Care Psychologist for several reality tv series. She is the author of several books on psychology and relationships.

'During the pandemic, I coached a lot of couples who were having a difficult time: couples who had had a perfectly good relationship when they saw each other briefly either side of work, but with lockdown they were plunged into something completely different with no escape from their partner. Throw in home-schooling and no wonder they found it tough.

I saw one couple who were spiralling quickly in the wrong direction. Their communication had lost a lot of its life; just informational stuff. "It's bin day tomorrow." "I'll cook pasta tonight." Often critical, "You haven't done the washing up yet". "Why are you on the phone all the time?" with a negative tone, often just a "look", and it would quickly become an argument.

The wife didn't work and had been pleased the husband was now working from home, hoping she would see him more. But in practice, he was so over-stretched, migrating the business to a remote operation and keeping it going in the face of the economic slowdown, that she actually saw him less. As she saw it, he was never off the phone, never off email, even when they went to bed he would be scrolling through his phone. Even when they did agree to set aside some time for a nice dinner, he would book it in his diary and she just felt it was like a business appointment. She felt neglected and this turned more and more to resentment and to arguments.

➤

On his part, he couldn't understand the fuss: "What could you be upset about? I'm the one who's working 15 hours a day so we can still afford this lovely house". All he saw, every time he looked up, was an angry woman nagging him, which just made him withdraw into his work even further. It became a vicious cycle.

And so they came to see me.

Now, my role isn't to instruct them, it's to guide. Let's say they've lost the connection, I'll take them back to the early days and ask "Why did you fall in love in the first place?". Then they'll come up with their own ideas: they might suggest looking back on some old holiday photos, this kind of thing. It's co-creation but their owning it means it will last a lot longer.

In this particular situation, the husband and wife had to understand the other better and why they were behaving like they were. But they had been too emotionally distant from each other so they hadn't been able to have this type of communication by themselves. But we got there.

She felt she was being neglected by her husband but it was as much being neglected by the circumstances. He, on the other hand, was so consumed by the immediate needs of his work, he had no clue he was neglecting her emotional needs.

She needed to understand why he seemed to be avoiding her and he needed to understand why she seemed to be so needy. So that's what we explored.

They agreed boundaries that both could be happy with. Things like banning the phone at dinner time, making bedtime their time. They found ways he could give her more time but didn't neglect his business.

On her part, she came to realise that constantly asking him when is he going to finish, does he want a cup of tea and so on, prolongs his day rather than helps matters. He now has less distraction, which means he can finish earlier so she, in turn, has more of him.

She also looked at what she could do to stave off the boredom of the pandemic. She couldn't go out for lunch with her friends anymore so she had to find something else to do. So she took up a new hobby, something creative (I won't say what it is for confidentiality reasons) but she enjoyed it and it kept her busy.

They were able to find their balance and they're now in a much better place. I told them they didn't really need me any more and they got upset; they thought I was breaking up with them!'

In summary

The best solution is always co-created because now both parties fully own it and will both work to make it a success.

- Treat it as a collaborative problem-solving process

  This will lead to the best results because the solution doesn't lie with any one of you, by working together you will find the optimal outcome. Plus, you will build a collaborative way of working together which will pay off many times in the future.

- Plan the process collaboratively too

  If you agree together the process ahead of time, things will go much more smoothly. And then, lead them through that process, checking in with them at each stage that they are still in agreement.

- Problem-solving is a highly creative activity

  Often it is difficult to identify the solution so in these instances you need to be creative. Identify as many variables as you can that can be brought into the negotiation and be inventive in coming up with possible answers.

- Stay focused on the vision

  Stand-offs usually occur because people are too fixated on the detail. But the detail, though important, is always secondary to the Why Five Times goal so if you focus on that (for both sides) you will find an answer that suits everyone.

- Don't fuel the fight

  Changing their mind will never happen if it's become a fight. You have to de-escalate and that usually means you taking the lead in this respect. So do what you need to de-escalate and only then can you have a proper conversation.

In this way, we find a solution that we know will be supported by everyone. But the content of the solution is one thing, how you present it is another. And that's what we will look at in Chapter 6.

6 Say it the right way

6.1 Right time, right place, right channel

Eight billion people, all different. So how do we know how to persuade that given person sitting in front of us right now? Well, all the work we've done in Chapters 1 through to 5 will tell us how.

The reason why our persuasion efforts usually fail is that, normally, we dive straight in with our advice, with our suggestions, with how they're wrong – and this just doesn't work. Sure, it's persuaded us, but that doesn't mean it will persuade them.

You will only change their mind if they are open to listening in the first place and if you have a solution that they are likely to accept, and all of that comes from the work done in the previous chapters.

And you also need to know how to put that solution across to that individual specifically: what will work with one person won't work for another – and, again, much of what we need for this comes from those earlier chapters.

Now in this chapter we'll look at what else we can do to make our communication most compelling.

And first off is choosing the right time, the right place and the right channel.

Find the right time

Niki Lauda, the three-times World Champion Formula One Racing Driver, was racing in 1978 for the Brabham team, owned by Bernie Ecclestone. Lauda was being paid £500,000 per year and wanted a pay-rise but Ecclestone refused and rang all the other teams to persuade them not to give him a better deal. Lauda had no choice but to accept his current salary.

For the time being, at least.

A short while later, he and Ecclestone met with the food giant Parmalat to discuss sponsorship. Parmalat asked who was driving. Ecclestone said Lauda, which gave Lauda his opportunity. Very calmly, Lauda said no he wasn't because he wasn't paid enough and Ecclestone was forced to increase the salary to £2 million, there and then, because he needed to ensure the sponsorship.[1,2]

Lauda waited for that key strategic moment where he knew his request would have most leverage, but sometimes it's simply about getting them in a good mood or a bad one. Professor Shai Danziger of Ben Gurion University conducted a study of over 1100 parole hearings in Israel and found a high correlation between the decision made and blood sugar levels: they were more likely to give parole if the decision was made shortly after food.[3]

Deciding on parole is an important and difficult decision and the default is to deny it. Any contrary decision would require a lot of thinking and this can only be done when their brain has sufficient fuel to do that thinking.

TOP TIP

If you want them to make the default decision, ask when they are tired and hungry. But if you need them to do more thinking, do it with or just after food.

Find the right place

The place can make a difference too, it can help set the right atmosphere. Do you want it to be formal or informal? Do you want it to be at their place or yours?

In 2012 when two of the largest commodities companies in the world, Glencore and Xstrata, were merging, the deal hit a significant stumbling block. The major shareholders of Xstrata, the royal family of Qatar, did not like the terms and conditions of the deal and were blocking it from going ahead.

So how was the situation resolved?

Well, it turns out the Qatar royal family were very good friends with Tony Blair, who was also good friends with the chief exec of Glencore, Ivan Glasenberg. So, they all met up for dinner at Claridge's, one of the best restaurants in London, and bashed it out. A multi-billion-dollar problem solved by good food and fine wine in a fancy restaurant.

Find the right channel

In recent years, the world has moved more and more online. This was true even before Covid-19, but the pandemic has accelerated it massively. So we now also have to consider the best channel.

Obviously online brings advantages – we can negotiate from anywhere on the planet. You could be typing away while sitting on the beach, you can include all parties and you don't have to organise everyone being in the same place at the same time.

It's tremendously convenient but this very convenience can be a problem too because email negotiations have their disadvantages.

For a start, it is much harder to explore topics, asking multiple questions in an open-ended, creative kind of way. So the solution reached is likely to be sub-optimal.

Plus, informationally it's a very diminished channel because so much of our communication is in the non-verbals: the facial expression, the tonality and so on. None of these is there in the email which means nuance, irony, sarcasm, humour and emotions do not convey and so the likelihood is that we communicated something different to what we intended.

Emails are famously easy to misinterpret and also tend to be less diplomatic. We see this in other online contexts like trolling where hiding behind a screen enables us to write things that we wouldn't normally say face-to-face and this then spirals out of control. One person writes something that they feel they need to say, the other person takes it in the wrong way and replies accordingly. Then the first person reads it and gets angry and slowly (often rapidly) it escalates. We have all been there.

And, finally, less trust is built through email and this can be fatal to the conversation. Human beings are social animals and we build trust through proximity. Research on negotiations shows that the remote deals fail more frequently than face-to-face and even if they reach an outcome, it is likely to be a sub-optimal outcome. It is something we really need to address if we want to get good results from our interactions.[4,5]

TOP TIP

If you do find your email conversation going downhill, the answer is usually very easy: pick up the phone.

Find the right blend

This isn't to say that email is bad. We just need to be aware that we are usually over-reliant on it as a channel because it is the most convenient. Instead, the best approach is a blended approach.

If it is at all possible, face-to-face is better. Human beings are pack animals and there is something very primal about meeting someone in terms of building trust. If we have met someone once, we are likely to trust them more; if we have met them twice, we are likely to trust them even more still. So use that.

Face-to-face is typically much less convenient though, so video conferencing is the next-best alternative. You can see and hear them so it is still a rich channel of communication but you can also work at a distance so you can schedule to meet your New York and your Indian colleagues at the same time. Failing that, use the telephone and keep emails for short factual communications or where you need an audit trail or where the logistics are too difficult to resolve.

Don't email simply because you always email. Each channel has its own advantages and disadvantages and you want to be aware of them and then choose consciously to best leverage their attributes.

And if it's not going well in any particular channel, change the channel. If your emails are getting nowhere, pick up the phone. If that still doesn't work out, meet face-to-face. Maybe try the coffee shop or the restaurant.

Maybe even Claridge's.

6.2 The best words are their words

As we saw in Chapter 5, getting them to create the answer is the key. If your ticket was specifically for the train that just left, asking them to let you on the next one might get a curt refusal. But if, instead, you tell them of the problem and let them come up with the answer, you might get 'Oh, don't worry about that, give me your ticket, I'm sure we can change it'.

We've now given them the opportunity of feeling good about themselves because (a) it was their solution and (b) they are doing a good deed. You never know, cognitive dissonance might even bump you into First Class!

If it's their idea, you're on to a winner. The 'not invented here' syndrome means if it's not their idea, they will probably fight against it; but if they think it is, they will fight *for* it.

And why not give them credit for it even if it *wasn't* their idea. So phrases like those below will get you a long way:

- 'As you said earlier. . . '
- 'I love your idea that. . . '
- 'Building on your earlier comment. . . '
- 'You've given me an idea. . . '.

Never let your ego get in the way of your outcome.

Persuade them with their words

Letting them come up with your answer is the ideal but it isn't always possible. If you are going to make a suggestion, though, keep it as close to their thinking as possible and the simplest way to do this is to use their words.

If they have used a specific word in a particular context, consciously or subconsciously they have chosen that word;

if we use any other word (a word we might think means the same), we are risking getting it wrong.

Them: What I need right now is a holiday.

Us: Yes, get away from it all.

Them: No, I'm not going anywhere, I'm just going to stay at home and chill.

If we'd just stuck with 'holiday', we would all have been in agreement.

Now, it is different if we need to check our understanding of something, in this instance we would use our own words: when our boss says he needs the report quickly, we might think by the end of the week is quite quick, they might think the end of the day. But for influencing purposes, using different words simply increases the chances they will disagree. We can be confident they won't disagree with their own words; anything else brings in doubt.

Persuade them how they told you to

If we don't use their exact words, at least use their style of words. While your impeccable logic is perfect for persuading yourself, it will not necessarily change anyone else's mind, so you need to put your message in terms of how they make their decisions.

For example, some people are risk-averse, others are 'go-getters'. To motivate the former, talk about the problems that will arise if they do not take this course of action. To motivate the latter, talk about the benefits that will accrue by taking it. This small change in emphasis will increase your chances of buy-in.

We've seen already in the book that people tell you how they make their decisions all the time. So, if you did your research in Chapter 2 and you listened deeply in Chapter 3, you will know exactly how to persuade them. This is the place where all that work pays off.

And then you work with these and you put your message in terms of these and it is more likely to get through.

As an example, researchers at UC Berkeley found that most pro-environmental arguments in the media were framed in terms of caring for the natural environment and protecting it. Now, these are values that resonate a lot more with liberals than with conservatives. Conservatives, however, were more likely to be enrolled by articles that stressed protecting the purity of the environment and which showed images of dirty drinking water and pollution.[6]

Along similar lines, Professor Christopher Wolsko of Oregon State University did a similar experiment where he gave participants two different messages, exhorting them to implement more environmentally friendly policies: the first appealing to care and compassion for the natural world, the second to the purity of the environment and to patriotism. Liberals were much more likely to respond to the former and conservatives to the latter.[7]

5 THINGS TO CONSIDER IN FORMULATING YOUR MESSAGE

1. Their drivers, what they want and don't want, their hopes and their fears.
2. Their emotions.
3. Their values.
4. Their criteria, the specific attributes that they are looking for in their choices.
5. Their personality type.

Sell it how they told you to

We can see how this works in sales. Perhaps you have a great product with lots of amazing features to set it apart from the competition. If you are lucky, you are talking to a technical person who will understand straightaway how they can use those features.

Most customers, though, do not buy on features. That amazing widget you're selling with an incredibly exciting tool for digging stones out of horses' hooves? The client doesn't care.

Spell out the value though, the value to that particular client in their specific current situation, and you have a sale.

- If they have told you they want to cut production time, tell them how this will cut production time, tell them by how much (based on figures they gave you) and then show how much money it will save them each quarter.
- If they have told you they are trying to get into a new market, tell them how these features will help break that market and remind them of how much the market is going to be worth in the next five years (again, based on figures they gave you).
- If they have mentioned a fear over the organisation's reputation, show how these features will bolster the reputation.
- If they once mentioned an interest in life after death, don't go that far, all claims must be ethical and based on facts but you get the idea.

And, by the way, it is your professional duty to do this. You are working with things that they have told you are important to them. And, surprisingly, they sometimes forget this. They will try to push you down on cost; they will say you are more expensive than your competitor. But all of this is a distraction from what is actually really important to them.

After all, the money saved by the reduction in production time will be much more than your costs. The value of the new market you will help them break into will be much more than your costs. The value of their reputation will be much more than your costs.

Keep them focused on this and they will buy from you.

TOP TIP

Link your outcomes to their personal goals too, their bonus or their promotion or simply how good they will look in front of their boss.

Persuade them with compelling words

And if we are using our own words, find the best ones. There is often a choice of words that will fit the context and one will be more compelling than the other. Choose that one.

The words we choose create a reality and so we want to create the most persuasive reality we can. Professor Elizabeth Loftus and John C Palmer, both of Washington University, showed people a video of a traffic accident and some people were asked, 'How fast were the cars travelling when they contacted the other car?' and others, '. . . when they smashed into the other car?'. The second group's estimate was nearly 30 per cent higher than that of the first group.[8]

Insurance companies have found that people pay twice as much for a medical policy that covers death 'by any disease' than they will for one that covers death 'by any reason', even though the latter includes the former. But it is less specific and therefore less vivid and therefore has less of an emotional impact.

6.3 Say the words they want to hear

Perhaps the best words are the words the other person wants to hear, the ones that make them look good.

Flattery has long been known to be a great influencer. Everyone likes to think they are rational and make their decisions based on the facts and logic; but throw in a few compliments, and their judgement is all over the place. We can't help but be charmed.

As Lady Randolph Churchill said, 'When I left the dining room after sitting next to Gladstone, I thought he was the cleverest man in England. But when I sat next to Disraeli I left feeling that I was the cleverest woman'.

No one is immune. In an article called 'The slime effect',[9] published in the *Journal of Personality and Social Psychology*, Roos Vonk showed that when we read flattering descriptions of other people, we often believe the flatterer was a slimeball. However, the same flattery written about ourselves is perceived as honest and insightful!

Asking advice from someone is an implicit form of flattery and this too will get them on your side. If you ask advice from your boss's boss, from your prospective client, from your negotiating counterparty, from that person of the opposite political persuasion, it can be a very effective way of getting them on your side.

Flattery has a bad name, though, so a sophisticated reader like yourself (did you see what I did there?) might not be comfortable with it. Let me suggest another word: complimenting. It's basically the same and much more socially acceptable. Complimenting is a key element of charm and charisma. And as long as you are authentic and honest with your praise, helping the other person feel good about themselves can only be a good thing.

Compliment their behaviour to get more of that behaviour

You've probably heard of Pudsey the dog, if not do look him up. Pudsey was a remarkable dog who performed on stage, was a guest judge on several television shows and even starred in a film. His career began when he won *Britain's Got Talent* in 2012. I always thought this was an indictment on Britain, that our best talent was a dog. But Pudsey was no ordinary dog: Pudsey danced, sang and recited the works of Shakespeare.

And Pudsey was trained using clicker training, a form of positive reinforcement that developed from the work of B.F. Skinner and Karen Pryor. Its basis is that if you reward a behaviour, you get more of that behaviour. The reward with dogs is initially a choccy drop and, later, a click. Dogs, not being too intelligent, seem to like clicks as much as choccy drops.

This method works for dogs and it also works for other animals like boyfriends, girlfriends, husbands, wives, bosses and so on. For these animals, though, a simple compliment is usually more advisable than a click or choccy drop.

Let me give an example from my own life. When I was 8 years old I played in an organised football team for the first time. At that age, there are no set positions for the players, just a scrum of kids following the ball around the pitch. I found myself at the edge of that scrum and I turned, found myself in space, and, as I remember, ran the length of the pitch and scored a brilliant goal. My memory is a little hazy, it has to be said, and the last bit might not be entirely true.

But what I do remember for certain is that my coach called out from the sidelines, 'Good turn, Simon' and I heard that and it stuck. 'I'm a good turner', I thought proudly and from then on, every time I got the ball, I turned. And turning in football, in general, is a good thing to do – you find space, you change direction, there is an element of surprise. His reinforcement of the behaviour with a compliment produced more of it.

You can even do it on something the other person doesn't do very often. Let me give you another example: I was once coaching someone on their public speaking and, as they practised an upcoming talk, they constantly walked from one side of the stage to the other which quickly became distracting so I thought it was a point I would raise.

Now, I could have told them to stop doing it, but many people are nervous about presentations and the last thing they need is something else to worry over and be self-critical about. So instead I said, 'There was one point in the middle where you stood still and looked me, the audience, in the eye. That was really powerful. Do a lot more of that'. So he did.

So if your neighbour is always playing the bagpipes at night, just compliment them for that moment when they were quiet.

Say 'no' by saying 'yes'

Typically people don't like to hear the word 'no': the word 'yes' is much more satisfying to hear.

Our experience of being told 'no' is rarely pleasant. It is actually like taking a physical hit – it's a painful experience, it triggers the amygdala and releases lots of stress-producing hormones and neuro-transmitters.

As such, it's not a word you should use lightly but, at the same time, we saw in Chapter 4 how important it is to have a strong 'no'.

So, if you can find alternative ways to say the same thing, that is often advisable. For example, saying 'no' to your boss can be extremely career-limiting and yet sometimes you have to, so being able to say it without causing offence is useful although not always easy.

A great way to say 'no' is to use the word 'yes' (with an important caveat on its way) and we've already seen in Chapter 5 the generative power of the phrase 'Yes and. . . '.

In fact, from one perspective, the answer is always 'Yes, if. . . '. In other words, your yes is conditional on something that you would like in return. This way, everybody can get their win. 'Yes, I'm happy to stay late tonight if I can leave early on Friday because I'm going away for the weekend.'

Now, to be fair, we haven't really said 'no', but we have used it to make sure we get something that we wouldn't have otherwise. Most things have their price, even if exorbitantly high. Use this method to get that cheeky price.

Sometimes, though, you really do need to refuse but without offending. And again the best way is to start with 'yes'. Then follow it up with something that you can agree to or acknowledge.

- 'Yes, that report does need to be finished tonight'.
- 'Yes, I understand why you say that and I would feel the same if I were in your shoes.'

Notice that although you've said 'yes', you haven't actually agreed to their request.

The next step is to give your reasons why you will have to decline and then say 'no'. It is important to do it in that order. If you say 'no' first, they will just hear the 'no' and won't hear the reasons. Give the reasons first, however, and they will hear them and be primed for the decline that follows.

Then finish off with another sweetener ('. . . I hope you get it sorted' or '. . . leave it on my desk and I will do it first thing tomorrow') and you've got across your refusal without losing the deal or the relationship.

So, putting it all together in an example for illustration: Let's say you're selling your beautiful car to a friend and they put the emotional squeeze on and ask you to knock off another 5 per cent because they're a good friend; don't say 'no', say, 'Yes, you're right, we go back a long way so I'm giving you the best deal I can, and I've already knocked off more than I should really so I'll have to stick to this figure this time. But you've got a fabulous car there at a great price. You'll love every moment you drive it'.

You can keep your friends, your job and your deal by knowing how to say 'no' smoothly.

Now, I said there was an important caveat on its way. In certain situations, your 'no' must be unequivocal and saying 'no' with the word 'yes' can be considered equivocal. Some people, minded to hear agreement, will pick up on the 'yes' and take it you've agreed.

I was reminded of this by a friend who had two teenage daughters and she was, of course, absolutely correct. So make sure you have an unmistakable categorical 'no' available to you when necessary; but in more diplomatically sensitive times, other language might be more befitting.

Use your customers' language

Danny Russell, Brand Insights Consultant. Danny has spent 28 years building expertise in strategic insight for major global brands including 21st Century Fox, Eir, The Economist *and Sky.*

'In those days, Sky was a bit of a machine that had its own way of doing things, but the world had changed and those things weren't really the right things to do any more. Our acquisition rates were going down, our cost of sales going up; we were saying the same things but people weren't responding.

So we had to change.

And I came up with the Customer Closeness Programme to get our senior management to go through the customer journey and understand what it was really like to be a customer on that journey.

Like a lot of companies, we had some very highly paid executives, ferried around in chauffeured cars, very intelligent, top of their game, but a million miles from their customer and they had lost touch with what it was like to be paying over £50 per month subscription on average wage.

So we got James Murdoch himself and his team to go round knocking on doors, talking to the customers, to find out what it was they were looking for. And they found some interesting things.

Within the organisation, Sky Sports was extremely powerful politically-speaking so a lot of our advertising was about football. But when we ran the Customer Closeness events with households we found the man, on his own, would say he was definitely going to sign up but, when the whole family were together, the wife would say they weren't. In fact, one man begged us to stop showing football in the adverts because his wife would always say "That's why we're not having Sky in our house".

So we devised a whole new campaign where we toned down the references to football and emphasised all our documentaries and nature programmes instead.

And we had a breakthrough with Sky Plus as well. It had been on the market for a while but people didn't seem to be getting the point of it. Then at one of the Customer Closeness events it became very clear that we got much better results when we removed the marketers from the conversation and, instead, let potential customers talk to existing ones.

> The marketers would always talk about how much more we had - more channels, more sports, more football - but people didn't really want more; they felt they were watching as much as they had time for anyway.
>
> The existing customers, though, were able to tell them it wasn't actually about more, it was about better. "It enables me to record just the things I want to watch and watch them when I want to watch them." Wow, why haven't the marketers told me this before!
>
> One particular customer was brilliant at it, she just naturally spoke the customers' language. We wanted to film her for a television advert and we got her to the studio but at the last moment she decided not to do it. So we got Michael Parkinson instead as a simple talking head to the camera. He was a customer and because he was homely, trustable Michael Parkinson saying why he thought Sky Plus was so great, it became one of our best performing ads ever.
>
> In the end, the Customer Closeness Programme was one of the main reasons that we were able to grow from seven million subscribers to our target of ten million within three years because we learnt to use our customers' language.'

6.4 What is your body saying?

So far in the book, we've learnt from ducks, squirrels and lobsters. In this last chapter, we will look to the great philosopher of the ocean – the cuttlefish.

Cuttlefish are remarkable creatures for many reasons including the facts they have three hearts, eight arms and two tentacles. None of them speaks English, however, and so we're specifically interested in how they communicate, especially the fact they communicate with their bodies.

In their skin, they have millions of pigment cells and so they can change their colours, chameleon-like, and this is how they communicate. Their 'language' has up to 75 chromatic elements and some cuttlefishologists believe their communication even has a grammar to it.

They can even change the texture of their skin, for example, making it spikey as a warning signal before a fight. In fact, during mating, the male can communicate different signals at the same time. The side closest to the female will have a smooth, lovingly romantic texture but if a rival wanders by, the side closest to the rival will be aggressively spikey.

Humans are nearly as intelligent as cuttlefish and we too communicate with our bodies. Less so with colour (although ever find yourself blushing?) but more with posture, gestures, facial expression and non-content attributes of voice.

In fact, your body language talks very loudly, so make sure it agrees with what you are saying.

Are you projecting the right status?

For a start, your body language conveys status and we saw in Chapter 4 how, for pack animals like humans, status is extremely important and the higher status you are, the more likely people will buy into your message. But status is not absolute, there is no grand register where you can check your innate status score – what counts in status is what is perceived and that, in turn, depends on what is projected.

So what status do you project? Do you walk timidly into the room, hoping not to be seen, talk quietly and rarely give strong eye contact? Or do you sit and stand tall, give a good handshake, lots of eye contact, and talk with a strong voice? Or are you leaning forward with unwavering eye contact, pointing fingers, banging tables and shouting?

TOP TIP

Make sure the status you are projecting is the Goldilocks status - *just right* for your situation, confident but not domineering - and communicate it with the appropriate body language.

Are you projecting credibility?

Linked to status is credibility. Do they believe you will deliver on your promise? Do they believe you believe what you are saying?

Deborah Tannen, Professor of Linguistics at Georgetown University, considered chief executives who often have to 'make decisions in five minutes about matters on which others may have worked five months'. How do they do this? As much on how confidently it is presented as on content.

Make your case and pack it with 'erms' and 'errs' and 'possiblys' and 'maybes', while shaking the head and looking down, and they simply won't buy into it, even if it is true. But back it up with lots of confident and assertive body language and they will sign up, even if the reality is not quite as straightforward as you suggest.

Are you projecting approachability?

Of course, it's not all about showing how strong and confident you are. The other side of the coin is communicating openness and approachability. Many people want to work with people they like and a positive relationship will definitely help your case.

And that is a whole different set of body language elements.

Smiling, lots of facial expression and head movement, lots of hand gestures and sentences finishing on the up (like an implied question-mark) all tend to suggest approachability and friendliness; in contrast to silence, lack of facial expression and movement and staring stony-faced back which people typically find uncomfortable to be with.

You can also build rapport by matching the other person's body language. Remember in Chapter 3 we looked at the work of Professor Uri Hasson and how he found the more people's brains were synchronised (the greater the neural entrainment, in other words), the better the conversation was judged to be?

Well, neurophysiologist Giacomo Rizzolatti discovered a part of the brain called mirror neurons that notice movement in other people and fire an impulse for the same movement in ourselves. They are the conduit by which the motor sections of the brain become synchronised. So if you match someone's posture, making similar gestures and generally following their lead in the non-verbals, the brains will become more entrained through the mirror neurons and, subconsciously, people will tend to feel more comfortable in your presence.

Don't copy, they'll think you're a freak

Now, obviously this is not to copy. If you overtly copy them, they will notice, start to edge away from you and think you're a freak! There is no quicker way to lose rapport. But there is a way of doing it artfully, so that you don't copy but, in some kind of way, you do something similar and this is what you should aim for.

That said, you will find most people are not consciously aware of body language or gestures, either theirs or yours, and consequently you have more margin to play with than you think before they think you're weird (unless, of course, you're weird).

And, indeed, sometimes you want to mismatch. If you want to close down a meeting, steer the conversation away from the current topic or subconsciously communicate disagreement with what is being said, mis-matching their behaviour can be the best way of doing it. It will communicate all of these without actually saying anything verbally.

Body language is the grandaddy of all languages: it persuades, it builds friends, it dances, it sings. Be like the cuttlefish. Use your body language to communicate and make sure it agrees with what you are saying.

6.5 Setting the right frame

Consider this thought experiment:

> Parallel universe 1: You are in a car boot sale and you come across a vase that you like and you decide to buy it. How much would you expect to pay?
>
> Parallel universe 2: You are in a mid-range department store and you come across the same vase. How much would you expect to pay here?
>
> Parallel universe 3: You are in a highly exclusive antiques store in the poshest part of town and you come across the same vase. How much would you expect to pay here?

This is a thought experiment, it is not real, but I imagine that you came up with very different prices for each setting, even though it was exactly the same vase. So how we value things depends a lot on the context.

Framing impacts our reality

This is the nature of framing – depending on how we look at things, we will view them differently. Let's take a look at a couple of examples.

- Is the glass half-full or half-empty? Take an empty glass and fill it up to half-way, 88 per cent will say it is half-full. Take a full glass and pour half of it out, only 31 per cent will say the same.[10]
- In a study where doctors considered the merits of surgery on cancer patients, of those that were told 10 out of 100 who went through surgery died, only half considered it a good option. Of those that were told 90 out of 100 survived surgery, 84 per cent thought it recommended.[11]

- If you are told a venture has a one-in-six chance of succeeding, you are far more likely to give it a go than if you are told it has a 16 per cent chance of success. And if you are told it is 84 per cent likely to fail, you just won't bother.

In each of these cases, we are presenting identical data differently, framing it differently, and so it receives a different evaluation and we give the vase a different price.

Professor Vernon Smith conducted an experiment where he got one group of people to negotiate with their 'opponents' and another with their 'partners'. The 'partners' got much better results than the 'opponents' because they were more collaborative. That's framing.[12]

We can manage the context within which the discussion takes place and thereby manage their perception and their reaction in order to get better results.

The price is itself a frame

The frame impacts our evaluation (for example, the price) but interestingly the price can, in turn, be part of the framing.

Take the vase:

- If you paid a few pounds for it at a car boot sale you would take it home but quite possibly never get around to putting it out on display.
- If you bought it from the mid-range department store and paid the corresponding price, you would probably put it on display in the kitchen or in the bathroom.
- But if you bought it from the exclusive antiques store and paid top-dollar for it, you would put it in pride of place in the middle of the dining table or by the front door so that everyone who comes around will see it.

Even though it is exactly the same vase. The price itself has impacted our evaluation.

So bear this in mind when you price your services. If you are cheap, you are communicating cheapness to the market; but if you have a top-end price, you are communicating a top-end service.

Now, you then have to make sure that you *deliver* a top-end service but your price is part of your brand and how people perceive you is impacted by your price.

Framing can impact your health

This is a very real physical effect. Dan Ariely conducted an experiment on the efficacy of a new painkiller. Volunteers were given electric shocks of varying intensity and were then given the tablet and asked to report any change in the level of pain.

Of those volunteers who were told the tablets cost 10 cents each, about half reported a reduction in pain level. Of those who were told they cost $2.50, nearly everyone did.

The 'painkiller' was actually a Vitamin C tablet.[13]

It can be even more tangible than that. Harvard psychologist Ellen Langer found that two-thirds of hotel chambermaids did not view their work as physical exercise, despite the fact that they are on their feet working hard all day.[14]

So she took 84 chambermaids and split them into two groups: one group was educated into the number of calories they burnt at work and how that work qualified as exercise, the other was left as the control.

After one month, both groups had their measurements taken again and the educated group had all lowered their weight, fat percentage and blood pressure while the control had all stayed the same. Framing their work as 'exercise' led to a measurable improvement in health.

Framing can be a very powerful way of changing how they see the situation and therefore their likely response.

Ownership is a frame

In an experiment where people were shown a mug, one group was asked how much they would buy the mug for (implying they did not own it already) and, on average, said $2.88. The second group of people were asked how much they would sell it for (implying they did own it already) and their average price was $7.12.[15]

Ownership is a frame – if I own it, I will value it higher than if I don't.

Now we can ascribe ownership by giving choice. Langer gave one group of people a lottery ticket each and allowed another group to choose their own. They were then instructed to sell the tickets: the group who had chosen theirs asked for four times the price than the other group.[16]

So, if we give choice, we give ownership; and if we give ownership, they will value it more.

This is a key aspect of persuasion. Let them choose. If we tell, they will likely fight against it; if we let them choose, they will fight *for* it.

So when your client asks you to provide a service for them, give them different options and let them choose. Perhaps your proposal outlines three ways of working:

> Option A: Full scope, full price
>
> Option B: Minimum scope, minimum price
>
> Option C: Something in between these two.

Whichever they choose, they will be more invested in it because it was their choice. Also, the cognitive bias is such that they normally choose Option C and will go away feeling they have negotiated and got a better deal, even though you haven't reduced your rate at all: you have just changed the price by changing the scope.

TOP TIP

Ascribe ownership by giving the option to say 'no'. If we add the comment 'Feel free to say "no"', then paradoxically they are less likely to.

Framing the sentence

Framing is useful at a micro-level too if, for example, you have something to say that may not be received well. It will be received better if you mention your intentions first.

The simplest example is if someone is talking and you would like to say something: the interruption will be more graciously indulged if you started with 'Sorry, can I interrupt?' or 'Can I ask a question?'.

By asking permission, you are giving them the opportunity to say 'no' even though it is exceedingly unlikely they will do so.

6 WAYS TO BROACH A SENSITIVE TOPIC

1. Can I ask a difficult question?
2. Do you mind if I say something you might find challenging?
3. I'd like to raise an issue I think is important. . .
4. I'm going to say something that could be mis-interpreted. . .
5. What I'm going to say next might come across as harsh. . .
6. There's just one point I'd like to disagree with, if I may. . .

In each of these situations, the upfront honesty and the request for permission will probably help it land more successfully. Of course, don't use it as an opener for some soul-crushing personal character assassination; but if it is authentically trying to progress the conversation, pre-framing a difficult statement with your intention will generally smooth its reception.

6.6 Telling the right story

People are rarely excited about listening to sales pitches, party political broadcasts or sermons of any kind and usually switch off very early on.

People love stories though. So tell a story and they will listen.

We have evolved to tell stories. We have the templates in our head, you just have to fit your content to the template.

And we have evolved to listen to them; we listen attentively wanting to know exactly what happens next. They are easy to understand and they are easy to remember because the templates provide the links between the different parts of the story.

When we listen, we live the experience of the story ourselves in a very real way – for example, reading the word 'lavender' activates the olfactory regions of the brain.

So they are powerful ways of changing minds.

Let's say your child comes back from school upset because they didn't do well in an exam. You could exhort them to work harder, but don't you think they've thought of that already? The logical answer isn't what's needed right now.

Instead, perhaps sit down alongside them on the sofa and listen to them fully and then tell them a story of how, when you were younger, you did badly in an exam and you felt just as bad as they did now. You had all kinds of setbacks but then at one point you realised there was no use in moping and so you picked yourself up and got down to some more work for the re-sit. In the end you got an A*.

Or remind them of the game when their favourite team was losing at half-time but they came back and turned it around.

Or simplest of all, watch *Rocky* together or *The Full Monty* or any of the million Hollywood films about triumph over adversity.

It's the story that will shift their mind much more powerfully than any advice.

Stories and the Vulcan Mind-Meld

When it comes to changing minds, the gold standard is undoubtedly the Vulcan Mind-Meld, first brought to human awareness by Mr Spock in the original series of *Star Trek*. And we saw in Chapter 3 how the work of Princeton Professor Uri Hasson showed that neural entrainment was, in fact, the basis of this process.

Perhaps that is a claim too far, but his work *does* show that the more closely the brains have become synchronised, the better the conversation is considered by its participants.

It turns out that telling stories is an extremely powerful way of linking brains. Not just the auditory areas of the brains, not just the linguistic areas and not just the areas encoding the factual components of the story either, but much higher-order areas too.

And these areas remain coupled as the story unfolds in an ongoing process of dynamic synchronisation, dancing together to the same beat and the same story.

9 THINGS THAT MAKE A GOOD STORY

1. They have interest, people want to listen because they want to hear what happens next.
2. There are surprises.

3. There is humour.
4. There is meaning.
5. There is struggle before success, failure before redemption.
6. They take the listener on an emotional journey.
7. They have personality, they have individuality.
8. They are personal. . .
9. . . . but they are universal too.

Tell them about the dream

Perhaps most of all, a good story will inspire.

Carmine Gallo, author of the best-selling *Talk Like TED*, says tell a story and start with your passion: if you can't inspire yourself, how will you inspire anyone else?[17]

He tells the story of how Clarence Jones, speech-writer for Martin Luther King, sat listening to King as he spoke to a crowd of 250,000 people from the steps of the Lincoln Memorial in Washington DC. 'Five score years ago', he began and Jones knew what was coming next because he wrote the speech.

Except for one thing. Standing very close to King was the gospel singer Mahalia Jackson and she called out, 'Tell them about the dream, Martin!'

King heard it and Jones heard it too. Jones watched King as he leaned back to look at the crowd. Jones whispered to the person next to him, 'These people out there don't know it yet but they're about to go to church'.

And Martin Luther King put aside his carefully crafted speech and, in full Baptist preacher mode, continued off-script: 'I have a dream. . . '.

If you can inspire with your story, you will change their mind; maybe you will change many minds.

I told them my story

David Villa-Clarke, BEM, Founder of DVC Wealth Management. He is also Chairman of Project Volunteer, a charity supporting projects in Africa for the last 15 years, and CEO of the Aleto Foundation, a social mobility charity providing leadership education for young people from under-privileged communities. David was awarded the British Empire Medal for his commitment to charitable services and mentoring.

'Last year I was asked by a new headmaster to help out at his inner-city school, which for the past four years had been ranked as "Requires improvement" by Ofsted and had seen four head teachers come and go within the same period.

It was in an area known for drug-dealing and with a high crime rate and he was expelling pupils at the rate of five per week to bring some order and discipline to the school.

I said I'd take 10 boys on a bootcamp to show them the opportunities that could be available to them. I didn't want the top, I didn't want the bottom, I wanted a mixture, and I needed to meet their parents as well.

The first meeting didn't start well. Several of the parents were late. There was only one father in the room. When I asked the kids how many of their parents talked to them about their homework, one and a half hands went up. You could tell the parents weren't fully sold on this, so why would the kids be? If you're a young black boy who doesn't have good role models around them, you'll find things to do and some of those things aren't good to do.

So I told them my story.

I told them I'm not a teacher, I'm not their father, I'm just someone who cares. And I think them seeing a black male, someone they could relate to, deemed to be successful, helped them buy into it. I told them I was from a similar background, working class parents, divorced, brought up in the 60s and 70s in Woolwich, a National Front stronghold. As a 9-year-old, I'd walk home from Cub Scouts and be chased by 17-year-old skinheads wanting to beat me up for being black.

I discovered tennis at 13 and found that I was good at it, and someone took me under their wing and gave me lessons and I went on from there.

Thanks to tennis, I was introduced to a different lifestyle and got to meet people from different social backgrounds from me, whose parents had white collar jobs and they lived a better lifestyle and didn't have to worry about paying bills.

I saw that there was a different route open to me. I worked in insurance for a while and then got a job in a prestigious property company based in Sloane Square, working with a bunch of people who had all been to the best finishing schools in Switzerland. I was mentored by the accounts director, which helped my career progress.

The point for the pupils was they saw a black male who they could identify with and hearing his story helped both the parents and the kids relate to the business bootcamp idea better. I had faced the same challenges that they bumped up against and I had managed to get around them.

So it turned them around and they signed up to the bootcamp. Our field trips were to a big bank in the city, a law firm event, and another finance company. I had motivational speakers in to talk to them, people who looked like them and were from their background. All opportunities they simply would not otherwise have had.

Of course, they had to put a lot of work in themselves. As part of the programme, the boys set their own ground rules that we would manage the project by – they needed to be well turned out, tie done up properly, shoes cleaned, no bad reports from the teachers, to have done their homework, and be good role models to their peers.

> And because they set their rules, they stood up for them: if someone broke them, others would point to the charter. Once, someone turned up to a review meeting with his tie undone because he had a bad hand and two others instantly jumped up to do it up for him.
>
> The net results? Well, a couple dropped out early but everyone else stayed the course and, in their exams, they all improved by at least one grade point and some by two.
>
> Most importantly of all, though, they saw possibilities open to them that they had not seen before.'

In summary

What persuades you is not necessarily the same as what persuades someone else. So you need to take care about how exactly you present your message to them.

- The when, where and how is important

  Pick your moment carefully: choose the time and place where they are most likely to be supportive of your message. And, despite its convenience, don't depend too much on email: phone or face-to-face will probably work much better.

- Work with what they give you

  Use their drivers, use their reasons, use their words. People are so helpful – they give you lots to work with; it would be impolite to use anything else. And it would certainly be less effective.

- Don't be an energy vampire

  People like being around people who help them feel good and they are more likely to be persuaded by such people too. So charm, compliment, say thanks, acknowledge their effort and say 'yes' much more than 'no'. Yes?

- Your body communicates too

  So make sure it agrees with you. Use your body language to project status, credibility and approachability. Humans have hundreds of millions of years of history where non-verbal communication was the *only* communication, so tap into that and use it to support what you are saying.

- Set the frame

  You can manage how someone sees a situation by how you frame it. This works at the conversation level (e.g., giving them a choice increases their chance of saying 'yes') or at the sentence level (e.g., asking permission to ask a sensitive question will help it be received more generously).

- Tell them a great story

  People love a good story so if you want them to listen, tell them a great story. They'll buy because of the story more than the logic.

And the great news is that most of what you need to succeed in this part of the process, you will have picked up from doing the work in Chapters 1–5. And if not, go through Chapters 1–5 again because there was probably something else you missed that will make all the difference when it comes to changing the other person's mind.

Afterword: Get better results, build better relationships, save the world

Most methods we use to persuade simply don't work.

Even those methods backed by millions of pounds in contexts of the very highest importance don't work. One systematic meta-analysis of 49 field experiments in political campaigning in US elections found their average effect in changing voters' minds to be approximately zero.

So we need to do something different if we want to be more effective.

Deep Canvassing: Listening them into it

We started our book with the 2009 vote in Maine that went against LGBT rights and was to be reversed 3 years later. At about the same time, the LGBT community had a similar setback in California when Proposition 8 was voted in, which effectively prohibited same-sex marriage.

David Fleischer became director of the Los Angeles LGBT Center shortly afterwards and decided to find out why. He and his team took to the streets and knocked on doors, not to persuade (it was too late for that), but to listen. And in doing so, he found that listening was able to persuade far better than any other approach he had taken before. The Deep Canvassing technique was born.

Political scientists David Broockman (University of California, Berkeley) and Josh Kalla (Yale) have run a number of studies on Deep Canvassing and it turns out to be remarkably successful.[1,2] They found in one study, in the context of the 2020 Trump/Biden election, that for every completed 100 conversations, 3.1 new votes for Biden were created. That might seem small but it was estimated at over 100 times more effective than a typical Presidential persuasion programme and would be enough to swing the result in nine different states in 2016.

What specifically does it involve? Well, instead of talking the voter into changing their mind, it works by *listening* them into it. The canvasser rapportfully and non-judgementally asks the voter their opinion on a topic and then asks lots of open questions around their experience on it, helping them reflect in an honest and analytical way. The canvasser will also share their own story.

So, by connecting through a common humanity, sharing stories and by allowing the voter to come to their own conclusion rather than be pressured into changing their mind, they get great success in changing people's minds on some very tough subjects.

But if you have read this far in the book you wouldn't be surprised by that at all.

Because Deep Canvassing really isn't that much different to Motivational Interviewing, the approach that works so well with addicts and repeat offenders. Or Disciplined Listening or Forensic Interviewing, the approach that works in police interrogations. Or the Behavioural Change Stairway, the hostage negotiator's go-to strategy. Each approach the same with a different name.

It really is remarkable that such different fields, each equally tough in their own way, have independently developed such similar strategies.

What has this got to do with tennis?

These are the techniques that work. These are the forehand and backhand of persuasion. Roger Federer (feel free to substitute Rafa Nadal, Novak Djokovic or Serena Williams if you prefer) has never invented any amazing new type of shot: he simply plays the forehand and the backhand – just the same as any other player.

Federer doesn't win every game, of course, but when he does it's with these shots and when he doesn't it's because he didn't play these shots well enough.

It's the same with changing someone's mind. Knowing your outcome, doing your research, listening, projecting strength, co-creating the solution and putting the message across in the right way for the other person – these are the basic shots of the game: the forehand and the backhand. These are the shots that work and you can get better and better at them and become more and more adept at persuading in ever more difficult situations.

Hopefully, dear reader, your persuasion conversations will rarely be as extreme as persuading addicts, terrorists or hostage takers and so the means described in this book should be perfectly adequate. That doesn't mean that you will always persuade everyone but, should you not, you just need to re-visit the methods and employ them better. Federer doesn't invent a new shot if he loses a game, he just plays the forehand and backhand better.

This beautiful broken planet

In 2010, I sat outside a café in Damascus, Syria, enjoying the air of a beautiful historic city, watching the locals go about their daily lives. A thought passed my mind that nearby Baghdad would have been such a city only ten years earlier and now it had been bombed to smithereens: so many lives, families, businesses and buildings destroyed.

As I watched the Damascenes chat and laugh and do their thing, it occurred to me that Baghdad folk would have been very similar, just normal sweet people wanting to get on with their lives; the very last thing they wanted was the devastation of war. And it occurred to me, too, that the same could happen here in Damascus and what a tragedy that would be.

A year later it happened.

We need to change how we work.

Let's do it now

And quickly.

We live in an accelerating world with technology begetting technology at an ever-faster rate. This is fantastic news. We have within our view a paradise on earth. We have the tools available to create a world of abundance for all; a world myths have been built on – Utopia, Eden, Arcadia, Shangri-La, however you want to call it. We can do it.

But it is dangerous news too. As the great biologist Edmund O. Wilson pointed out, we have Paleolithic brains, mediaeval institutions and god-like technology. This is not a healthy combination. Our power is enormous; we have to learn to use it better. We are such an amazing species that has done so many incredible things in our short history. But whether it is war, climate change, the catastrophic collapse of nature or winner-takes-all capitalism, we can be so destructive too.

We are the sub-species Homo sapiens sapiens – sapiens means wise and we are named it twice. Let's live up to it for our own good.

The minds, they are a-changin'

Currently, outside of violence and coercion, there are three prevailing methods of persuasion:

- Shouting, as seen in social media
- Manipulation, as seen in online sales and advertising
- Lying, as seen in politics.

No wonder our planet is at breaking point.

The great news is that there is a method that works better and it is the method you have read about in these pages. These approaches will get people talking constructively, not destructively; they will get people to open up not close down; they will heal wounds, not deepen them; they will bridge divides, not widen them.

They can take us down the path we really want to go down.

But even if you don't care about the rest of the world, even if you only care about that centre of the universe that is you, this approach will do you best. Because not only does it bring you better outcomes, but it also brings you better relationships.

Outcomes and relationships, this is your life.

This is your career, the house you live in, your holidays; this is your colleagues, your friends, the people around you; this is your loved ones, your children, your family.

This is your life.

You can change their mind, you can change many minds, and you will get better results and you will build better relationships as you do so. So in getting good at this, you get good at your life and help everyone around you get good at theirs too.

You may even save the world at the same time.

May the road rise with you.

References

Chapter 1 Aim high

1 MacDonald, K. (2008) *One Red Paperclip: The Story of How One Man Changed His Life One Swap at a Time*. Kyle MacDonald, Ebury Press.

2 See www.telegraph.co.uk/women/mother-tongue/6559883/Families-spend-four-days-a-year-arguing.html (accessed 5 January 2022).

Chapter 2 Look for clues

1 Matz, S.C. and Harari, G.M. (2020) Personality–place transactions: mapping the relationships between big five personality traits, states, and daily places. *Journal of Personality and Social Psychology: Personality Processes and Individual Differences* 120(5): 1367–1385. www.gwern.net/docs/psychology/personality2020-matz.pdf

2 North, A., Hargreaves, D. and McKendrick, J. (1997) In-store music affects product choice. *Nature* 390: 132. https://doi.org/10.1038/36484

3 Mitchell, G. (1999) *Making Peace: The Inside Story of the Making of the Good Friday Agreement*. William Heinemann.

4 Levine, M., Prosser, A., Evans, D. and Reicher, S. (2005) Identity and emergency intervention: how social group membership and inclusiveness of group boundaries shape helping behavior. *Personality & Social Psychology Bulletin* 31: 443–453. https://doi.org/10.1177/0146167204271651

5 Hirsh, J., Kang, S. and Bodenhausen, G. (2012) Personalized persuasion: tailoring persuasive appeals to recipients' personality traits. *Psychological Science* 23: 578–581. https://doi.org/10.1177/0956797611436349

6 https://www.academia.edu/9995428/The_paradox_of_project_control

Chapter 3 Listen, listen, listen

1 Derber, C. (2000) *The Pursuit of Attention: Power and Ego in Everyday Life*. Oxford University Press.

2 Kaplan, J., Gimbel, S. and Harris, S. (2016) Neural correlates of maintaining one's political beliefs in the face of counterevidence. *Scientific Reports* 6, 39589. https://doi.org/10.1038/srep39589

3 Zajonc, R.B. (1980) Feeling and thinking: preferences need no inferences. *American Psychologist* 35(2): 151–175. https://doi.org/10.1037/0003-066X.35.2.151

4 See www.nytimes.com/2016/02/28/magazine/what-google-learned-from-its-quest-to-build-the-perfect-team.html (accessed 10 January 2022).

5 Alison, E. and Alison, L. (2020) *Rapport: The Four Ways To Read People.* Vermilion.

6 Lieberman, M.D., Eisenberger, N.I., Crockett, M.J., Tom, S.M., Pfeifer, J.H. and Way, B.M. (2007) Putting feelings into words: affect labeling disrupts amygdala activity in response to affective stimuli. *Psychological Science* 18(5): 421–428.

7 Shapiro, D. (2016) *Negotiating the Nonnegotiable: How to Resolve Your Most Emotionally Charged Conflicts.* Penguin Books.

8 Morwitz, V., Johnson, E. and Schmittlein, D. (1993) Does measuring intent change behavior? *Journal of Consumer Research* 20(1): 46–61. www.jstor.org/stable/2489199

9 Greenwald, A.G., Carnot, C.G., Beach, R. and Young, B. (1987) Increasing voting behavior by asking people if they expect to vote. *Journal of Applied Psychology* 72(2): 315–318. https://doi.org/10.1037/0021-9010.72.2.315

10 Huang, K., Yeomans, M., Brooks, A.W., Minson, J. and Gino, F. (2017) It doesn't hurt to ask: question-asking increases liking. *Journal of Personality and Social Psychology* 113(3): 430–452. https://doi.org/10.1037/pspi0000097

11 Yi Hu, Yinying Hu, Xianchun Li, Yafeng Pan and Xiaojun Cheng (2017) Brain-to-brain synchronization across two persons predicts mutual prosociality. *Social Cognitive and Affective Neuroscience* 12(12): 1835–1844.

12 Stephens, G.J., Silbert, L.J. and Hasson, U. (2010) Speaker–listener neural coupling underlies successful communication. *Proceedings of National Academy of Sciences USA* 107(32): 14425–14430. https://doi.org/10.1073/pnas.1008662107

13 Smirnov, D., Saarimäki, H., Glerean, E., Hari, R., Sams, M. and Nummenmaa, L. (2019) Emotions amplify speaker–listener neural alignment. *Human Brain Mapping* 40(16): 4777–4788. https://doi.org/10.1002/hbm.24736

Chapter 4 Be strong

1 Arreguín-Toft, I. (2005) *How the Weak Win Wars: A Theory of Asymmetric Conflict*. Cambridge Studies in International Relations Book 99, Cambridge University Press.

2 Noesner, G. (2010) *Stalling For Time: My Life as an FBI Hostage Negotiator*. Random House.

3 Zak, P. (2013) *The Moral Molecule: How Trust Works*. Plume Books.

4 John, L.K. (2016) How to negotiate with a liar. *Harvard Business Review*, July–August 2016.

5 Lee, F., Peterson, C. and Tiedens, L. (2004) Mea culpa: predicting stock prices from organizational attributions. *Personality and Social Psychology Bulletin* 30(12): 1636–1649.

6 Ho, B. and Liu, E. (2011) Does sorry work? The impact of apology laws on medical malpractice. *Journal of Risk and Uncertainty* 43: 141–167.

7 Halperin, B., Ho, B., List, J. and Muir, I. (2022) Toward an understanding of the economics of apologies: evidence from a large-scale natural field experiment. *The Economic Journal* 132(641): 273–298.

8 Dalio, R. (2017) *Principles: Life and Work.* Simon & Schuster.

9 Tetlock, P. and Gardner, D. (2016) *Superforecasting: The Art and Science of Prediction.* Random House.

Chapter 5 Co-create the solution

1 See www.england.nhs.uk/wp-content/uploads/2017/04/ppp-involving-people-health-care-guidance.pdf (accessed 6 January 2022).

2 Zartman, W. and Faure, G. (2011) *Engaging Extremists: Trade-offs, Timing and Diplomacy.* United States Institute of Peace Press.

3 Grenny, J., Patterson, K., Maxfield, D., McMillan, R. and Switzler, A. (2013) *Influencer: The New Science of Leading Change.* McGraw-Hill.

4 Osborn, A. (1942) *How To Think Up.* McGraw-Hill.

5 Osborn, A. (1963) *Applied Imagination: Principles and Procedures of Creative Problem Solving.* Charles Scribner's Sons.

6 Blas, J. and Farchy, J. (2021) *The World For Sale: Money, Power and the Traders Who Barter the Earth's Resources.* Oxford University Press.

7 Lax, D. and Sebenius, J. (1986) *The Manager as Negotiator: Bargaining for Cooperation and Competitive Gain.* The Free Press.

8 Shapiro, D. (2016) *Negotiating the Nonnegotiable: How to Resolve Your Most Emotionally Charged Conflicts.* Penguin Books.

9 Stone, D., Patton, B. and Heen, S. (2011) *Difficult Conversations: How to Discuss What Matters Most.* Penguin.

Chapter 6 Say it the right way

1 Watkins, S. (2010) *Bernie: The Biography of Bernie Ecclestone.* Haynes Publishing.

2 See www.youtube.com/watch?v=haCMlpDKxLk (accessed 6 January 2022).

3 Danziger, S., Levav, J. and Avnaim-Pesso, L. (2011) Extraneous factors in judicial decisions. *Proceedings of the National Academy of Sciences USA* 108(17): 6889–6892. https://doi.org/10.1073/pnas.1018033108

4 Valley, K.L. (2000) The electronic negotiator: negotiations over email. *Harvard Business Review* 78(1) (January–February): 16–17. Reprint F00103.

5 Parlamis, J. and Ames, D. (2010) Face-to-face and email negotiations: a comparison of emotions, perceptions and outcomes. *SSRN Electronic Journal.* https://doi.org/10.2139/ssrn.1612871

6 Feinberg, M. and Willer, R. (2012) The moral roots of environmental attitudes. *Psychological Science* 24(1): 56–62. https://doi.org/10.1177/0956797612449177

7 Wolsko, C., Ariceaga, H. and Seiden, J. (2016) Red, white, and blue enough to be green: effects of moral framing on climate change attitudes and conservation behaviors. *Journal of Experimental Social Psychology* 65: 7–19.

8 Loftus, E.F. and Palmer, J.C. (1974) Reconstruction of automobile destruction: an example of the interaction between language and memory. *Journal of Verbal Learning and Verbal Behavior* 13(5): 585–589.

9 Vonk, R. (1998) The slime effect: suspicion and dislike of likeable behavior toward superiors. *Journal of Personality and Social Psychology* 74: 849–864. https://doi.org/10.1037/0022-3514.74.4.849

10 McKenzie, C.R.M. and Nelson, J.D. (2003) What a speaker's choice of frame reveals: reference points, frame selection, and framing effects. *Psychonomic Bulletin & Review* 10: 596–602. https://doi.org/10.3758/BF03196520

11 Tversky, A. and Kahneman, D. (1986) Rational choice and the framing of decisions. *The Journal of Business* 59(4): Part 2, S251–S278.

12 Burnham, T., McCabe, K. and Smith, V. (2000) Friend-or-foe intentionality priming in an extensive form trust game. *Journal of Economic Behavior & Organization* 43: 57–73. https://doi.org/10.1016/S0167-2681(00)00108-6

13 Ariely, D. (2009) *Predictably Irrational: The Hidden Forces That Shape Our Decisions*. Harper.

14 Crum, A.J. and Langer, E.J. (2007) Mind-set matters: exercise and the placebo effect. *Psychological Science* 18(2): 165–171.

15 Kahneman, D., Knetsch, J.L. and Thaler, R.H. (1990) experimental tests of the endowment effect and the Coase theorem. *Journal of Political Economy* 98(6): 1325–1348. https://doi.org/10.1086/261737

16 Langer, E.J. (1975) The illusion of control. *Journal of Personality and Social Psychology* 32: 311–328.

17 Gallo, C. (2017) *Talk Like TED: The 9 Public Speaking Secrets of the World's Top Minds*. Pan.

Afterword: Get better results, build better relationships, save the world

1 Kalla, J.L. and Broockman, D.E. (2018) The minimal persuasive effects of campaign contact in general elections: evidence from 49 field experiments. *American Political Science Review* 112(1): 148–166.

2 Broockman, D. and Kalla, J. (2016) Durably reducing transphobia: a field experiment on door-to-door canvassing. *Science* 352(6282): 220–224.

Index